# Ireland in Po

Seven Hundred A.D. – T\ ␣␣␣ A.D.
Featuring The Poetry of Jam␣ ␣arence Mangan
and a Collection of Irish Poems and Songs
by Noted Poets and Songwriters of the Past

**Selected and Annotated**
by Robert Skelly

**Layout and Arrangement**
by Carol Kimberly

**Cover Photography**
by Tim Skelly, Australia

*Published by Donemark*

*Cover, Design and Printed
by Rayfount Digital Printers, Coventry*

Robert Skelly

# Ireland
## in poetry and song

Poetry is an excellent lesson in history and the ancient poetry of Ireland contains in every verse a story of our Country's glorious past, from the times of St Patrick, Brian Boru, Cahal Mór, the Great Earls of Ulster, O'Neill and O'Donnell, Sarsfield, the rebellions of the seventeenth and eighteenth century. The exceptional translations of James Clarence Mangan, the beautiful poetry of such as Thomas Moore, Michael Scanlan, Aubrey De Vere, Lady Dufferin, and a host of other wonderful poets and songwriters. Most of our poetry is sad and poignant, but if the time is taken to try to comprehend the message and meaning, they tell of glories and heartbreaks of our sometimes wonderful and sometimes tragic past.

It tells the lives of the times of our ancient and more recent heroes and their patriotism and sacrifice, for love of their native land. The lamentations are in some cases over one thousand years old. The lament for Kincora by McLiag, who was a secretary to Brian Boru, he died in 1015, a year after the Battle of Clontarf, is a very graphic description of the famous Kings and Lords of that time. In later times Boolavogue and Kelly of Killane, are a history lesson in themselves in the rising of 1798.

O'Donnell Abu, tells of the Great Earls of Ulster in the times of Queen Elizabeth the First and the plantations of Ulster.

Dark Rosaleen, Roisin Dubh and Kathaleen Ny Houlahan, tell the sorrows and hopes of Ireland in times of oppression and penal laws.

I sincerely hope you will enjoy this effort to bring to Irish people and young people of Irish descent, more understanding of our beloved Country, and its glorious past.

Robert Skelly

# Contents

*Introduction*          **7**

*Part One – The Poetry of James Clarence Mangan*       **9**

DARK ROSALEEN       11

THE WOMAN OF THREE COWS       14

KATHALEEN NY-HOULAHAN       16

THE DREAM OF JOHN MAC DONNELL       17

A LAMENTATION       20

LAMENT       22

THE DAWNING OF THE DAY       28

LAMENT FOR BANBA       29

CEAN-SALLA       31

ST. PATRICK'S HYMN BEFORE TARA       32

THE CAPTIVITY OF THE GAELS       36

ENTHUSIASM       38

THE SORROWS OF INNISFAIL       39

THE IRISH LANGUAGE       40

LAMENT FOR OWEN ROE O'NEILL       43

THE RUINS OF DONEGAL CASTLE       45

A FAREWELL TO PATRICK SARSFIELD, EARL OF LUCAN       47

ROISIN DUBH       50

SOUL AND COUNTRY       52

A VISION OF CONNAUGHT IN THE THIRTEENTH CENTURY       54

THE WARNING VOICE       56

IRISH NATIONAL HYMN                                   59

TO MY NATIVE LAND                                     61

THE DYING ENTHUSIAST                                  63

LINES ON THE DEATH OF A BELOVED FRIEND                65

TWENTY GOLDEN YEARS AGO                               67

THE COMING EVENT                                      69

COUNSEL TO THE WORLDLY-WISE                           71

COUNSEL OF A COSMOPOLITAN                             72

REST ONLY IN THE GRAVE                                73

THE NIGHT IS FALLING                                  74

THE GERALDINE'S DAUGHTER                              75

THE SONG OF GLADNESS                                  77

THE FAIR HILLS OF EIRE, O!                            79

OWEN REILLY: A KEEN                                   81

WELCOME TO THE PRINCE OF OSSORY                       84

LAMENTATION OF MAC LIAG FOR KINCORA                   86

A LULLABY                                             88

PRINCE ALFRID'S ITINERARY THROUGH IRELAND             91

ELLEN BAWN                                            94

RURY AND DARVORGILLIA                                 95

A HIGHWAY FOR FREEDOM                                 99

NOONDAY DREAMING                                      101

LINES WRITTEN IN A NUNNERY CHAPEL                     102

WISDOM AND FOLLY                                      103

KATHLEEN NI HOULAHAN *(Another Version)*              104

## Part Two – A selection of Famous Irish Poems and Songs by Noted Poets and Songwriters.                    **105**

| | |
|---|---|
| THE "WILD GEESE" | 106 |
| THE LAMENT OF THE IRISH EMIGRANT | 107 |
| CUISLE MO CHROIDHE | 109 |
| THE OLD LAND | 110 |
| SHE IS FAR FROM THE LAND | 111 |
| A BALLAD OF ATHLONE | 112 |
| NATIONALITY | 113 |
| MICHAEL DWYER | 115 |
| FLAG OF SINN FEIN | 117 |
| BOOLAVOGUE | 118 |
| ASPIRATIONS OF YOUTH | 119 |
| THE BELLS OF SHANDON | 120 |
| THE MINSTREL BOY | 122 |
| THE JACKETS GREEN | 123 |
| LET ERIN REMEMBER | 124 |
| O'DONNELL ABU | 125 |
| THE BATTLE EVE OF THE BRIGADE | 127 |
| GOUGAUNE BARRA | 128 |
| MY GRAVE | 130 |
| SALUTATION TO THE KELTS | 131 |
| KELLY OF KILLANNE | 132 |
| THE RECONCILIATION | 133 |
| FAR- AWAY | 134 |
| A GAELIC SONG | 135 |
| THE WEST'S ASLEEP | 137 |
| THE OLD LAND | 138 |

THIS IS MY OWN MY NATIVE LAND 139

THE LITTLE BLACK ROSE 140

THE EXILE'S DEVOTION 141

EXILE OF ERIN 142

RICH AND RARE WERE THE GEMS SHE WORE 144

THE BOLD FENIAN MEN 145

BANTRY BAY 146

THE LONDONDERRY AIR 147

## Part Three – Memories of an Exile 149

452 AD 150

GOOD FRIDAY 10-4-1014 AD 150

1-5-1170 150

4-9-1607 151

15-08-1649 151

MAY 1798 152

1800S 152

EASTER 1916 153

1919-1921 153

SEPTEMBER 1921 153

A CHILDHOOD DREAM 154

IRELAND 155

WHY 156

INNISFREE 157

THE WILD GEESE 1691 158

THE LONELY EMIGRANT 159

IRELAND'S LAMENT 160

# Introduction

## PART ONE

The Poems of James Clarence Mangan are in many cases translations from ancient Irish Poetry, and in some cases there are two versions, both of which are included, for instance, Roisin Dubh, is an earlier version of Dark Rosaleen, they are both mystic names for Ireland, and translate as Little Black Rose. Roisin Dubh was said by Mangan to have been written in the reign of Queen Elizabeth 1, by one of the Bards of Red Hugh O'Donnell Earl of Tyrconnell, and is supposed to be addressed to Ireland by that famous chieftain. Most of the ancient poems were unrhymed, Mangan worked on these and turned them into the beautiful poems which we read today. Many of his poems are Irish history lessons and tell wonderful stories of the past such as, Cahal Mór of the Wine-Red Hand, a King in Ireland in the Thirteenth Century, from whom the Red Hand of Ulster originated. Mangans A Vision of Connaught portrays him. There are two versions of Kathleen Ni Houlahan, another mystic name for Ireland, that in their own way are outstanding poems, and a tribute to Mangan's genius.

It gives one great pleasure to be able to go back hundreds of years in history to read and enjoy the wonderful poetry, and to try to appreciate the time and effort he had to put into his translations, considering the very limited facilities available to him in the early nineteenth century, as opposed to what is available to us today. His poem 'My Dark Rosaleen' was regarded as one of the finest lyrics in the world , and would have assured Mangan of everlasting fame even if he had not written much else.

Little is known of Mangan's family except that his Father was a native of Shanagolden Co Limerick, who in 1801 married Catharine Smith of Fishamble Street Dublin, in 1803 Mangan was born in the same street, his Father was a grocer, and was unfortunate in his business. Mangan was a shy and sensitive person, but had a fantastic sensibility to the beauty of the world, music and to the glory of heaven, and earth. He was humble, gentle, and modest. For seven years he slaved as a copyist in a scrivener's office for a paltry wage, he also worked as a clerk in an attorney's office. He devoted himself to unlocking the poetic treasures in foreign languages, he must have spent long nights reading, and writing poetry. He was not seen for some time, and eventually emerged a withered and stricken old man, he died in the Meath Hospital Dublin on 20 June 1849 of cholera, some say starvation, some say exhaustion aged forty-six. He is buried in an unmarked grave in Glasnevin Cemetery Dublin, next to the graves of the Plunkett Family for whom he worked as a clerk prior to his death.

I sincerely hope you enjoy this collection of Irish verse and song, a tribute to the wonderful Irish poets and songwriters of the past.

## PART TWO

The poems and songs have been carefully selected from famous Irish and Scottish poets and songwriters written mostly in the eighteenth and nineteenth centuries, and are wonderful examples of Irish and Celtic verse and song.

## PART THREE

Part three contains nostalgic memories of an exile of Ireland.

# PART ONE

# The Poetry
## of
## James Clarence Mangan

*James Clarence Mangan*

# DARK ROSALEEN

*(from the Irish of Costello)*

Oh My Dark Rosaleen
Do not sigh, do not weep!
The priests are on the ocean green,
They march along the Deep.
There's wine ... from the royal Pope
Upon the ocean green;
And Spanish ale shall give you hope,
My Dark Rosaleen!
My own Rosaleen!
Shall glad you heart, shall give you hope,
Shall give you health, and help, and hope,
My Dark Rosaleen.

Over hills and through dales
Have I roamed for your sake;
All yesterday I sailed with sails
On river and on lake.
The Erne .... at its highest flood
I dashed across unseen,
For there was lightning in my blood,
My Dark Rosaleen!
My own Rosaleen!
Oh! there was lightning in my blood,
Red lightning lightened through my blood,
My Dark Rosaleen!

All day long in unrest,
To and fro, do I move,
The very soul within my breast
Is wasted for you, love!
The heart in my bosom faints
To think of you, my Queen,
My life of life, my saint of saints,
My Dark Rosaleen!
My own Rosaleen!
To hear your sweet and sad complaints,
My life, my love, my saint of saints,
My Dark Rosaleen!

Woe and pain, pain and woe
Are my lot night and noon,
To see your bright face clouded so,
Like to the mournful moon,
But yet ... I will rear your throne
Again in golden sheen;
'Tis you shall reign and reign alone,
My Dark Rosaleen!
My own Rosaleen!
'Tis you shall have the golden throne,
Tis you shall reign, and reign alone,
My Dark Rosaleen!

Over dews, over sands
Will I fly for your weal;
Your holy delicate white hands
Shall girdle me with steel.
At home ... in your emerald bowers,
From morning's dawn to e'en,
You'll pray for me, my flower of flowers,
My Dark Rosaleen!
My fond Rosaleen!
You'll think of through Daylight's hours,
My virgin flower, my flower of flowers,
My Dark Rosaleen!

I could scale the blue air,
I could plough the high hills
Oh, I could kneel all night in prayer,
To heal your many ills!
And one ... beamy smile from you
Would float like light between
My toils and me, my own, my true,
My Dark Rosaleen!
My fond Rosaleen!
Would give me life and soul anew,
A second life, a soul anew,
My Dark Rosaleen!

O! The Erne shall run red
With redundance of blood,
The earth shall rock beneath our tread,
And flames wrap hill and wood,
And gun-peal, and slogan cry,
Wake many a glen serene,
Ere you shall fade, ere you shall die,
My Dark Rosaleen!
My own Rosaleen!
The Judgment Hour must first be nigh,
Ere you can fade, ere you can die,
My Dark Rosaleen!


Dark Rosaleen ('Ireland') is one of the finest lyrics in the language; it rankes with the best lyrics of the world. As the poet of 'Dark Rosaleen' alone Mangan would be assured of fame, even if he had not written much else.

*There's wine, etc* = money sent by the Pope to Ireland.
*Spanish ale* = probably means men and ammunition from Spain.
*Lightning in my blood* = his intense patriotism in the face of all danger and toil.
*Slogan* = war cry or gathering cry of the Gaelic Clans.

Mangan says this poem was entitled in the original Roisin Dubh, written in the reign of Elizabeth 1 by one of the poets of Red Hugh O'Donnell, and is supposed to be addressed to Ireland by that famous Chieftan.

# THE WOMAN OF THREE COWS

O, Woman of Three Cows, agragh![1] don't let your tongue thus rattle!
O, don't be saucy, don't be stiff, because you may have cattle
I have seen – and, here's my hand to you, I only say what's true -
A many a one with twice your stock not half so proud as you.

Good luck to you, don't scorn the poor, and don't be their despiser,
For worldly wealth soon melts away, and cheats the very miser,
And death soon strips the proudest wreath from haughty human brows;
Then don't be stiff, and don't be proud, good Woman of Three Cows!

See where Momonia's[2] heroes lie, proud Owen More's[3] descendents,
Tis they that won the glorious name, and had the grand attendants.
If they were forced to bow to Fate, as every mortal bows,
Can you be proud, can you be stiff, my Woman of Three Cows!

The brave sons of the Lord of Clare, they left the land to mourning;
Mavrone[4], for they were banished, with no hope of their returning -
Who knows in what abodes of want those youths were driven to house?
Yet you can give yourself these airs, O Woman of Three Cows!

O, think of Donnell of the Ships, the Chief whom nothing daunted,
See how he fell in distant Spain, unchronicled, unchanted,
He sleeps, the great O' Sullivan, where thunder cannot rouse -
Then ask yourself, should you be proud, good Woman of Three Cows!

O'Ruark, Maguire, those souls of fire, whose names are shrined in glory -
Think how their high achievements once made Erin's highest glory -
Yet now their bones lie mouldering under weeds and cypress boughs,
And so, for all your pride, will yours, O Woman of Three Cows!

The O'Carrolls[5], also, famed when Fame was only for the boldest,
Rest in forgotten sepulchres with Erin's best and oldest;
Yet who so great as they of yore in battle or carouse?
Just think of that, and hide your head, good Woman of Three Cows!

Your neighbour's poor, and you, it seems, are big with vain ideas,
Because, inagh[6], you've got three cows, one more, I see, than she has.
That tongue wags more at times than charity allows,
But, if you're strong, be merciful, great Woman of Three Cows

The Summing Up

Now, there you go!  You still, of course, keep up your scornful bearing,
And I'm too poor to hinder you; but, by the cloak I'm wearing,
If I had but four cows myself, even though you were my spouse,
I'd thwack you well to cure your pride, my Woman of Three Cows!

This ballad rebukes the saucy pride of a woman in the humble life who puts on airs of consequence, because she was the possessor of three cows. The name of the author is unknown. Translated from the Irish by James Clarance Mangan.

(1) Agragh (my dear)  (2) Momonia (Munster)  (3) Owen More (King of Munster) who, early in he second century, defeated Conn of the hundred battles  (4) Mavrone (my grief)  (5) The O'Carrolls (Lords of Ely, S.W. of Offally)  (6) inagh (is it not).

# KATHALEEN NY-HOULAHAN[1]

*(From the Irish of William Heffernan)*

Long they pine in weary woe, the nobles of our land,
Long they wander to and fro, proscribed, alas! and banned;
Feastless, houseless, altarless, they bear the exile's brand,
But their hope is in the coming-to of Kathaleen Ny-Houlahan!

Think her not a ghostly hag, too hideous to be seen,
Call her not unseemly names, our matchless Kathaleen;
Young she is, and fair she is, and would be crowned a queen,
Were the king's son at home here with Kathaleen Ny-Houlahan!

Sweet and mild would look her face, O, none so sweet and mild,
Could she crush the foes by whom her beauty is reviled;
Woollen plaids would grace herself and robes of silk her child,
If the king's son were living here with Kathaleen Ny-Houlahan!

Sore disgrace it is to see the Arbitress of thrones,
Vassal to a *Saxoneen* of cold and sapless bones!
Bitter anguish wrings our souls – with heavy sighs and groans
We wait the Young Deliverer of Kathaleen Ny-Houlahan!

Let us pray to him who holds Life's issues in His hands –
Him who formed the mighty globe, with all its thousand lands;
Girding them with seas and mountains, rivers deep, and strands,
To cast a look of pity upon Kathaleen Ny-Houlahan!

He, who over sands and waves led Israël along –
He, who fed, with heavenly bread, that chosen tribe and throng –
He, who stood by Moses,when his foes were fierce and strong –
May he show forth His might in saving Kathaleen Ny-Houlahan.

[1] A name by which Ireland was allegorically known.

# THE DREAM OF JOHN MAC DONNELL

*(From the Irish of John Mac Donnell, Clarach)*

I lay in unrest old thoughts of pain,
That I struggled in vain to smother,
Like midnight spectres haunted my brain-
Dark fantasies chased each other;
When, lo! a figure – who might it be-
A tall fair figure stood near me!
Who might it be? an unreal Banshee?
Or an angel sent to cheer me?

Though years have rolled since then, yet now
My memory thrillingly lingers
On her awful charms, her waxen brow,
Her pale, translucent fingers,
Her eyes that mirrored a wonder world,
Her mien of unearthly mildness,
And her waving raven tresses that curled
To the ground in beautiful wildness.

'Whence comest thou, spirit?' I asked, methought;
'Thou art not one of the Banished!'
Alas, for me! she answered nought,
But rose aloft and evanished;
And a radiance, like to a glory, beamed
In the light she left behind her,
Long time I wept, and at last medreamed
I left my shieling to find her.

And first I turned to the thunderous North,
To Cruagach's mansion kingly;
Untouching the earth I then sped forth
To Inver-lough, and the shingly
And shining strand of the fishful Erne,
And thence to Cruachan the golden,
Of whose resplendent palace ye learn
So many a marvel olden -

I saw the Mourna's billows flow-
I passed the walls of Shenady,
And stood on the hero-thronged Ardroe,
Embosked amid greenwoods shady;
And visited the proud pile that stands
Above the Boyne's broad waters,
Where Aengus dwells, with his warrior bands
And the fairest of Ulster's daughters.

To the halls of Mac Lir, to Creevroe's height,
To Tara, the glory of Erin,
To the fairy palace that dances bright
On the peak of the blue Cnocfeerin,
I vainly hied. I went west and east-
I travelled seaward and shoreward-
But thus was I greeted at field and at feast-
'Thy way lies onward and forward!'

At last I reached I wist not how,
The royal towers of Ival,
Which under the cliff's gigantic brow,
Still rise without a rival;
And here were Thomond's chieftains all,
With armour, and swords, and lances,
And here sweet music filled the hall
And damsels charmed with dances.

And here, at length, on a silvery throne,
Half seated, half reclining,
With forehead white as the marble stone,
And garments so starrily shining,
And features beyond the poet's pen-
The sweetest, saddest features-
Appeared before me once again,
The fairest of Living Creatures!

'Draw near, O! mortal' she said with a sigh,
'And hear my mournful story!
The guardian-spirit of Erin am I,
But dimmed is mine ancient glory;
My priests are banished, my warriors wear
No longer victory's garland;
And my Child[1], my Son, my beloved Heir,
Is an exile in a far land!

I heard no more - I saw no more -
The bands of slumber were broken;
And palace and hero, and river and shore,
Had vanished, and left no token.
Dissolved was the spell that had bound my will
And my fancy thus for a season;
But a sorrow therefore hangs over me still,
Despite the teachings of reason!

[1] The Young Pretender

# A LAMENTATION

*For the Death of Sir Maurice Fitzgerald*
*Knight of Kerry* [1]
*(From the Irish of Pierce Ferriter)*

There was lifted up one voice of woe,
One lament of more than mortal grief,
Through the wide South to and fro,
For a fallen chief.
In the dead of night that cry thrilled through me,
I looked out upon the midnight air!
Mine own soul was all as gloomy,
And I knelt in prayer.

O'er Loch Gur, that night, once – twice - yea, thrice -
Passed a wail of anguish for the Brave
That half curdled into ice
Its moon-mirroring wave.
Then uprose a many-toned wild hymn in
Choral swell from Ogra's dark ravine,
And Mogeely's Phantom Women [2]
Mourned the Geraldine!

Far on Carah Mona's emerald plains
Shrieks and sighs were blended many hours,
And Fermoy in fitful strains
Answered from her towers.
Youghal, Keenalmeaky, Eemokilly
Mourned in concert, and their piercing keen
Woke to wondering life the stilly
Glens of Inchiqueen.

From Loughmoe to Yellow Dunanore
There was fear; the traders of Tralee
Gathered up their golden store,
And preparerd to flee;
For, in ship and hall from night till morning
Showed the first faint beamings of the sun,
All the foreigners heard the warning
Of the Dreaded One!

"This," they spake, "portendeth death to us,
If we fly not swiftly from our fate!"
Self conceited idiots! Thus
Ravingly to prate!
Not for base-born higgling Saxon trucksters
Ring laments like those by shore and sea!
Not for churls with souls of hucksters
Waileth our Banshee!

For the high Milesian race alone
Ever flows the music of her woe!
For slain heir to bygone throne,
And for Chief laid low!
Hark! - Again, methinks, I hear her weeping
Yonder! Is she near me now, as then?
Or was't but the night-wind sweeping
Down the hollow glen?

[1] Who was killed in Flanders in 1642
[2] Banshees

# LAMENT

*For the Princes of Tyrone
and Tyrconnell (Buried in Rome)*

*(From the Irish of Hugh MacWard)*

O Woman of the piercing Wail,
Who mournest o'er yon mound of clay
With sigh and groan,
Would God thou wert among the Gael!
Thou wouldst not then from day to day
Weep thus alone.
Twere long before, around a grave
In green Tirconnell, one could find
This loneliness;
Near where Beann-Boirche's banners wave
Such grief as thine could ne'er have pined
Companionless.

Beside the wave, in Donegall,
In Antrim's glens, or fair Dromore,
Or Killilee,
Or where the sunny waters fall,
At Assaroe, near Erna's shore,
This could not be.
On Derry's plains - in rich Drumclieff -
Throughout Armagh the Great, renowned
In olden years,
No day could pass but Woman's grief
Would rain upon the burial-ground
Fresh floods of tears!

O, no! from Shannon, Boyne, and Suir,
From high Dunluce's castle-walls,
From Lissadil,
Would flock alike both rich and poor,
One wail would rise from Cruchan's halls
To Tara's hill;
And some would come from Barrow-side,
And many a maid would leave her home

On Leitrim's plains,
And by melodious Banna's tide,
And by the Mourne and Erne, to come
And swell thy strains!

O, horses hoofs would trample down
The Mount whereon the martyr-saint
Was crucified.
From glen and hill, from plain and town,
One loud lament, one thrilling plaint,
Would echo wide.
There would not soon be found, I ween
One foot of ground among these bands
For museful thought,
So many shriekers of the keen
Would cry aloud and clap their hands,
All woe distraught!

Two princes of the line of Conn
Sleep in their cells of clay beside
O' Donnell Roe;
Three royal youths, alas! are gone,
Who lived for Erin's weal, but died
For Erin's woe!
Ah! could the men of Ireland read
The names these noteless burial-stones
Display to view,
Their wounded hearts afresh would bleed,
Their tears gush forth again, their groans
Resound anew!

The youths whose relics moulder here
Were sprung from Hugh, high Prince and Lord
Of Aileach's land.
Thy noble brothers, justly dear,
Thy nephew, long to be deplored
By Ulster's bands.
Theirs were not souls wherein dull times
Could domicile Decay or house
Decrepitude!
They passed from earth ere Manhood's prime,

Ere years had power to dim their brows
Or chill their blood.

And who can marvel o'er their grief,
Or who can blame thy flowing thy flowing tears,
That knows their source?
O'Donnell, Dunnasava's chief,
Cut off amid his vernal years,
Lies here a corse
Beside his brother Cathbar, whom
Tirconnell of the Helmets mourns
In deep despair-
For valour, truth, and comely bloom,
For all that greatens and adorns,
A peerless pair.

O, had this twain, and he, the third,
The Lord of Mourne, and Niall's son,
Their mate in death-
A prince in look, in deed, and word-
Had these three heroes yielded on
The field their breath,
O, had they fallen on Criffan's plain,
There would not be a town or clan
From shore to sea
But would with shrieks bewail the Slain,
Or chant aloud exulting rann
Of jubilee!

When high the shout of battle rose,
On fields where Freedom's torch still burned
Through Erin's gloom,
If one, if barely one of those
Were slain, all Ulster would have mourned
The hero's doom!
If at Athboy, where hosts of brave
Ulidian horsemen sank beneath
The shock of spears,
Young Hugh O'Neill had found a grave,
Long must the North have wept his death
With heart-wrung tears!

If on the day of Ballach-myre
The Lord of Mourne had met, thus young,
A warriors fate,
In vain would such as thou desire
To mourn, alone, the champion sprung
From Niall the Great!
No marvel this-for all the Dead,
Heaped on the field, pile over pile,
At Mallach-brack,
Were scarce an eric for his head,
If Death had stayed his footsteps while
On victory's track!

If on the Day of Hostages
The fruit had from the parent bough
Been rudely torn
In sight of Munster's bands Mac-Nee's
Such blow the blood of Conn, I trow,
Could ill have borne.
If on the day of Ballach-boy
Some arm had laid, by foul surprise,
The chieftain low,
Even our victorious shout of joy
Would soon give way to rueful cries
And groans of woe!

If on the day the Saxon host
Were forced to fly-a day so great
For Ashanee
The Chief had been untimely lost,
Our conquering troops should moderate
Their mirthful glee.
There would not lack on Lifford's day,
From Galway, from the glens of Boyle,
From Limerick's towers,
A marshalled file, a long array
Of mourners to bedew the soil
With tears in showers!

If on the day a sterner fate
Compelled his flight from Athenree,
His blood had flowed,
What numbers all disconsolate
Would come unasked, and share with thee
Affliction's load!
If Derry's crimson field had seen
His life-blood offered up, though twere
On Victory's shrine,
A thousand cries would swell the keen,
A thousand voices in despair
Would echo thine!

Oh, had the fierce Dalcassian swarm
That bloody night on Fergus banks,
But slain our Chief,
When rose his camp in wild alarm
How would the triumph of his ranks
Be dashed to grief!
How would the troops of Murbach mourn
If on the Curlew Mountain's day,
Which England rued,
Some Saxon hand had left them lorn,
By shedding there, among the fray,
Their princes blood!

Red would have been our warrior's eyes
Had Roderick found on Sligo's field
A gory grave,
No Northern Chief would soon arise
So sage to guide, so strong to shield,
So swift to save.
Long would Leith-Cuinn have wept if Hugh
Had met the death he often dealt
Among the foe;
But, had our Roderick fallen too,
All Erin must, alas! have felt
The deadly blow!

What do I say? Ah, woe is me!
Already we bewail in vain
Their fatal fall!
And Erin, once the Great and Free,
Now vainly mourns her breakless chain,
And iron thrall!
Then, daughter of O'Donnell! dry
Thine overflowing eyes, and turn
Thy heart aside!
For Adam's race is born to die,
And sternly the sepulchral urn
Mocks human pride!

Look not, nor sigh, for earthly throne,
Nor place thy trust in arm of clay
But on thy knees
Uplift thy soul to God alone,
For all things go their destined way
As He decrees.
Embrace the faithful Crucifix,
And seek the path of pain and prayer
Thy Saviour trod;
Nor let thy spirit intermix
With earthly hope and worldly care
Its groans to God!

And thou, O mighty Lord! whose ways
Are far above our feeble minds
To understand,
Sustain us in these doleful days,
And render light the chain that binds
Our fallen land!
Look down upon our dreary state,
And through the ages that may still
Roll sadly on,
Watch Thou o'er hapless Erin's fate,
And shield at least from darker ill
The blood of Conn.

*Keen* = Funeral lament. *Rann* = Song. *Eric* = A fine or tribute.
*Ashanee* = Ballyshannon. *Leith-Cuinn* = the Northern part of Ireland.

# THE DAWNING OF THE DAY

*(From the Irish of O'Doran)*

'Twas a balmy summer morning
Warm and early,
Such as only June bestows;
Everywhere the earth adorning,
Dews lay pearly
In the lily-bell and rose.
Up from each green leafy bosk and hollow
Rose the blackbirds pleasant lay,
And the soft cuckoo was sure to follow.
'Twas the dawning of the day!

Through perfumed air the golden
Bees flew round me:
Bright fish dazzled from the sea,
Till me dreamt some fairy olden
World- spell bound me in a trance of witcherie.
Steeds pranced round anon with stateliest housings,
Bearing riders prankt in rich array,
Like flushed revellers after wine-carousings -
'Twas the Dawning of the Day!

Then a strain of song was chanted,
And the lightly floating sea-nymphs drew anear.
Then again the shore seemed haunted
By hosts brightly clad, and wielding shield and spear!
Then came the battle-shouts and onward rushing
Swords and chariots, and a phantom fray.
Then all vanished; the warm skies were blushing
In the Dawning of the Day!

Cities girt with glorious gardens
Whose immortal habitants in robes of light
Stood, methought, as angel-wardens
Nigh each portal, now arose to daze my sight.
Eden spread around, revived and blooming;
When, lo! As I gazed all passed away-
I saw but black rocks looming
In the dim chill Dawn of Day!

# LAMENT FOR BANBA [1]

*(From the Irish of Egan O'Rahilly)*

O My land! O my love!
What a woe, and how deep,
Is thy death to my long mourning soul!
God alone, God above,
Can awake thee from sleep,
Can release thee from bondage and dole!
Alas, alas, and alas!
for the once proud people of Banba!

As a tree in its prime,
Which the axe layeth low,
Didst thou fall, O unfortunate land!
Not by Time, nor thy crime,
Came the shock and the blow.
They were given by a false felon hand!
Alas, alas, and alas!
For the once proud people of Banba!

O, my grief of all griefs,
Is to see how thy throne
Is usurped, whilst thyself art in thrall!
Other lands have their chiefs,
Have their kings, thou alone
Art a wife, yet a widow withal!
Alas, alas, and alas!
For the once proud people of Banba!

The high house of O'Neill
Is gone down to the dust,
The O'Brien is clanless and banned;
And the steel, the red steel,
May no more be the trust
Of the Faithful and Brave in the land!
Alas, alas, and alas!
For the once proud people of Banba!

True, alas! Wrong and Wrath
Were of old all too rife.
Deeds were done which no good man admires:
And perchance Heaven hath
Chastened us for the strife
And the blood-shedding ways of our sires!
Alas, alas, and alas!
For the once proud people of Banba!

But, no more! This our doom,
While our hearts yet are warm,
Let us not over-weakly deplore!
For the hour soon may loom
When the Lord's mighty hand
Shall be raised for our rescue once more!
And our grief shall be turned into joy
For the still proud people of Banba!

[1] Banba was one of the most ancient names given by the Bards to Ireland.

# CEAN-SALLA

*The Last Words of Red Hugh O'Donnell on his
Departure from Ireland for Spain (from the Irish)*

Weep not the brave Dead!
Weep rather the Living
On them lies the curse
Of a doom unforgiving!
Each dark hour that rolls,
Shall the memories they nurse,
Like molten hot lead,
Burn into their souls
A remorse long and sore!
They have helped to enthral a
Great land evermore,
They who fled from Cean-Salla!

Alas, for thee, slayer
Of the kings of the Norsemen!
Thou land of sharp swords,
And strong kerns and swift horsemen!
Land ringing with song!
Land, whose abbots and lords,
Whose Heroic and Fair,
Through centuries long,
Made each palace of thine
A new western Walhalla
Thus to die without sign
On the field of Cean-Salla;

My ship cleaves the wave -
I depart for Iberia
But, oh! with what grief,
With how heavy and dreary a
Sensation of ill!
I should welcome a grave:
My career has been brief,
But I bow to God's will!
Yet if now all forlorn,
In my green years, I fall, a
Long exile I mourn -
But I mourn for Cean-Salla!

# ST. PATRICK'S HYMN BEFORE TARA[1]

*(From the Irish)*

At Tara to-day, in this awful hour,
I call on the Holy Trinity!
Glory to Him who reigneth in power,
The God of the elements, Father and Son,
And Paraclete Spirit, which Three are the One,
The ever-existing Divinity!

At Tara today I call on the Lord,
On Christ the Omnipotent Word,
Who came to redeem from Death and Sin
Our fallen race;
And I put and I place
The virtue that lieth and liveth in
His Incarnation lowly,
His Baptism pure and holy,
His life of toil, and tears, and affliction,
His dolorous Death  -  His Crucifixion,
His Burial, sacred and sad and lone,
His Resurrection to life again.
His glorious Ascension to Heaven's high Throne,
And, lastly, his future dread
And terrible coming to judge all men -
Both the Living and Dead. . . .

At Tara to-day I put and I place
The virtue that dwells in the Seraphim's love,
And the virtue and grace
That are in the obedience
And unshaken allegiance
Of all the Archangels and angels above,
And in the hope of the Resurrection
To everlasting reward and election,
And in the prayers of the Fathers of old,
And in the truths the Prophets foretold,
And in the Apostles' manifold preachings,
And in the Confessors' faith and teachings,

And in the purity ever dwelling
Within the Immaculate Virgin's breast,
And in the actions bright and excelling
Of all good men, the just and the blest. . . .

At Tara to-day, in this fateful hour,
I place all Heaven with its power,
And the sun with its brightness,
And the snow with its whiteness,
And fire with all the strength it hath,
And lightning with its rapid wrath,
And the winds with their swiftness along their path,
And the sea with its deepness,
And the rocks with their steepness,
And the earth with its starkness,[2]
All these I place,
By God's almighty help and grace,
Between myself and the Powers of Darkness.

At Tara to-day
May God be my stay!
May the strength of God now nerve me !
May the power of God preserve me!
May God the Almighty be near me!
May God the Almighty espy me !
May God the Almighty hear me!
May God give me eloquent speech!
May the arm of God protect me!
May the wisdom of God direct me!
May God give me power to teach and to preach!

May the shield of God defend me!
May the host of God attend me,
And ward me,
And guard me,
Against the wiles of demons and devils,
Against the temptations of vices and evils,
Against the bad passions and wrathful will
Of the reckless mind and the wicked heart
Against every man who designs me ill,
Whether leagued with others or plotting apart!

In this hour of hours,
I place all those powers
Between myself and every foe,
Who threaten my body and soul
With danger or dole,
To protect me against the evils that flow
From lying soothsayers' incantations,
From the gloomy laws of the Gentile nations,
From Heresy's hateful innovations,
From Idolatry's rites and invocations,
Be those my defenders,
My guards against every ban,
And spells of smiths, and Druids, and women;
In fine, against every knowledge that renders
The light Heaven sends us dim in
The spirit and soul of Man!
May Christ, I pray,
Protect me to-day
Against poison and fire
Against drowning and wounding,
That so, in His grace abounding,
I may earn the Preacher's hire!


Christ, as a light,
Illumine and guide me!
Christ, as a shield, o'ershadow and cover me
Christ be under me! Christ be over me!
Christ be beside me
On left hand and right!
Christ be before me, behind me, about me!
Christ this day be within and without me!


Christ, the lowly and meek,
Christ, the All-powerful, be
In the heart of each to whom I speak,
In the mouth of each who speaks to me!
In all who draw near me,
Or see or hear me!

At Tara to-day, in this awful hour,
I call on the Holy Trinity!
Glory to Him who reigneth in power,
The God of the Elements, Father and Son,
And Paraclete Spirit, which Three are the One,
The ever-existing Divinity!

Salvation dwells with the Lord,
With Christ, the Omnipotent Word.
From generation to generation,
Grant us, O Lord, thy grace and salvation!

[1] The original Irish text is in the Liber Hymnorum, in Trinity College, and is in the oldest form of dialect.

[2] "Properly" "strength," "firmness," from the Anglo-Saxon, *stark*, "strong; stiff:"

# THE CAPTIVITY OF THE GAELS

*(From the Irish)*

'Twas by sunset . . . I walked and wandered
Over hill-sides . . . and over moors,
With a many sighs and tears.
Sunk in sadness . . . I darkly pondered
All the wrongs our . . . lost land endures
In these latter night-black years.
"How," I mused, "has her worth departed!
What a ruin . . . her fame is now!
We, once freest of the Free,
We are trampled . . . and broken-hearted;
Yea, even our Princes . . . themselves must bow
Low before the vile Shane Bwee!"[1]

Nigh a stream, in . . . a grassy hollow,
Tired, at length, I . . . lay down to rest -
There the birds and balmy air
Bade new reveries . . . and cheerier follow
Waking newly . . . within my breast
Thoughts that cheated my despair.
Was I waking . . . or was I dreaming?
I glanced up, and . . . behold! there shone
Such a vision over me !
A young girl, bright . . . as Erin's beaming
Guardian spirit-now sad and lone,
Through the spoiling of Shane Bwee !

O, for pencil . . . to paint the golden
Locks that waved in . . . luxuriant sheen
To her feet of stilly light!
(Not the Fleece . . . in ages olden
Jason bore o'er . . . the ocean green
Into Hellas, gleamed so bright.)
And the eyebrows . . . thin arched over
Her mild eyes, and . . . more, even more
Beautiful, methought, to see,
Than those rainbows . . . that wont to hover
O'er the blue island-lakes of yore
Ere the spoiling by Shane Bwee !

"Bard!" she spake, "deem . . . not this unreal.
I was niece of . . . a Pair whose peers
None shall see on earth again -
AEongus Con, and . . .the Dark O'Niall,[2]
Rulers over . . . Iern in years
When her sons as yet were Men.
Times have darkened . . . and now our holy
Altars crumble, . . . and castles fall ;
Our groans ring through Christendee.
Still, despond not ! He comes, though slowly
He, the Man, who shall disenthral
The Proud Captive of Shane Bwee ! "

Here she vanished; . . . and I, in sorrow,
Bent with joy, rose . . . and went my way
Homeward over moor and hill.
O Great God! Thou . . . from whom we borrow
Life and strength, unto Thee I pray!
Thou, who swayest at Thy will
Hearts and councils, . . . thralls, tyrants, freemen,
Wake through Europe . . . the ancient soul,
And on every shore and sea,
From the Blackwater to the Dniemen,
Freedom's Bell will . . . ere long time toll
The deep death-knell of Shane Bwee !

[1] *Seagan Buidhe*, Yellow John, a name applied first to the Prince of Orange, and afterwards to his adherents generally.
[2] Niall Dubh

# ENTHUSIASM

Not yet trodden under wholly,
Not yet darkened,
Oh, my spirit's flickering lamp, art thou!
Still, alas! thou wanest - though but slowly;
And I feel as though my heart had hearkened
To the whispers of despondence now.

Yet the world shall not enthral me-
Never! never!
On my briary pathway to the grave
Shapes of pain and peril may appal me,
Agony and ruin may befal me-
Darkness and dismay may lower ever,
But, cold world, I will not die thy slave!

Underneath my foot I trample
You, ye juggles -
Pleasure, passion, thirst of power and gold!
Shall I, dare I, shame the bright example,
Beaming, burning in the deeds and struggles
Of the consecrated few of old?

Sacred flame-which art eternal!
Oh! bright essence!
Thou, Enthusiasm! forsake me not!
Oh, though life be reft of all her vernal
Beauty, ever let thy magic presence
Shed its glory round my clouded lot.

# THE SORROWS OF INNISFAIL

*(From the Irish of Geoffrey Keating)*

Through the long drear night I lie awake, for the sorrows of Innisfail.
My bleeding heart is ready to break; I cannot but weep and wail,
Oh, shame and grief and wonder! her sons crouch lowly under
The footstool of the paltriest foe that ever had wrought them woe!

How long O mother of light and song, how long till they fail to see
That men must be bold, no less than strong, if they truly will to be free?
They sit but in silent sadness, while wrongs that should rouse them to madness,
Wrongs that might rise the very Dead, are on thy devoted head!

Thy castles, thy towers, thy palaces proud, thy stately mansions all,
Are held by the knaves who crossed the waves to lord it in Brian's hall.
Britannia, alas ! is portress in Cobhthach's Golden Fortress'
And Ulster's and Momonia's lands are in the Robber- stranger's hands.

The tribe of Eoghan is worn with woe; the O'Donnell reigns no more;
O'Neill's remains lie mouldering low on Italy's far-off shore;
And the youths of the Pleasant Valley are scattered and cannot rally,
While foreign Despotism unfurls its flag mid hordes of base-born churls.

The Chieftains of Naas were valorous lords, but their valour was crushed by Craft
They fell beneath Envy's butcherly dagger and Calumny's poisoned shaft,
A few of their mighty legions yet languish in alien regions,
But most of them, the Frank, the Free, were slain by Saxon perfidie!

Oh ! lived the Princes of Ainy's plains, and heroes of green Domgole,
And the chiefs of the Maigue, we still might hope to baffle our doom and dole,
Well then might the dastards shiver who herd by the blue Bride river,
But ah ! those great and glorious men shall draw no glaive on Earth again!

All powerful God! look down on the tribes who mourn throughout the land,
And raise them some deliverer up, of a strong and smiting hand!
Oh! suffer them not to perish, the race thou wert wont to cherish,
But soon avenge their father's graves, and burst the bond that keeps them slaves!

# THE IRISH LANGUAGE

*(From the Irish of Philip Fitzgibbon)*

### I.

The language of Erin is brilliant as gold;
It shines with a lustre unrivalled of old.
Even glanced at by strangers to whom 'tis unknown
It dazzles their eyes with a light all its own!

### II.

It is music, the sweetest of music, to hear;
No lyre ever like it enchanted your ear.
Not the lute, or the flute, or the quaint clarionet,
For deep richness of tone could compete with it yet!

### III

It is fire to the mind-it is wine to the heart
It is melting and bold  -  it is Nature and Art!
Name one other language, renowned though it be,
That so wakes up the soul, as the storm the deep sea!

### IV.

For its bards  -  there are none in cell, cottage, or hall,
In the climes of the haughty Iberian and Gaul,
Who despair not to match them  -  their marvelful tones
Might have won down the gods of old Greece from their thrones!

### V.

Then it bears back your spirit on History's wings
To the glories of Erin's high heroes and kings,
When the proud name of Gael swelled from ocean to shore,
Ere the days of the Saxon and Northman of yore.

### VI.

Is the heart of the land of this tongue undecayed?
Shall the Sceptre and Sword sway again as they swayed?
Shall our Kings ride in triumph o'er war-fields again,
Till the sun veils his face from the hosts of the slain?

## VII.

O, then shall our halls with the Gaelic resound,
In the notes of the harp and the *claoirseach*[1] half drowned,
And the banquet be spread, and the chess-board all night
Test the skill of our Chiefs, and their power for the fight.

## VIII.

Then our silken-robed minstrels, a silver haired band,
Shall rewake the young slumbering blood of the land,
And our bards no more plaintive on Banba's dark wrongs,
Shall then fill *two* worlds[2] with the fame of their songs.

## IX.

And the gates of our *Brughaidhs*[3] again shall stand wide,
And their cead mile failte woo all withinside,
And the travel-tired wayfarer find by the hearth
Cheery Plenty where now, alas! all is Black Dearth.

## X

The down-trodden Poor shall meet kindness and care,
And the Rich be as happy to spare and to share!
And the Mighty shall rule unassailed in their might,
And all voices be blent in one choir of delight!

## XI.

The bright Golden Era that poets have sung
Shall revive, and be chaunted anew in our tongue;
The skies shall rain Love on the land's breadth and length,
And the grain rise like armies battalioned in strength.

## XII.

The priest and the noble, the serf and his lord,
Shall sustain one another with word and with sword-
The Learned shall gain more than gold by their lore,
And all Fate took away she shall trebly restore.

## XIII.

Like rays round a centre, like stars round the moon,
Like Ocean round Earth, when it heaves in the noon,
Shall our chiefs, a resplendent and panoplied ring,
In invincible valour encircle their King.

## XIV.

And thou, O Grand Language, please Heaven, shalt win
Proud release from the tomb thou art sepulchred in.
In palace, in shieling, on highway, on hill,
Shalt thou roll as a river, or glide as a rill!

## XV.

The story of Eire shall shine forth in thee;
Thou shall sound as a horn from the lips of the Free;
And our priests in their forefathers' temples once more
Shall through Thee call on men to rejoice and adore!

[1] Bagpipes. [2] Viz., America and Europe. [3] Public Victuallers.

# LAMENT FOR OWEN ROE O'NEILL

*(from the Irish of O'Daly)*

O mourn, Erin, mourn!
He is lost, he is dead,
By whom thy proudest flag was borne,
Thy bravest heroes led!
The night winds are uttering
Their orison of woe,
The raven flaps his darkling wing
O'er the grave of Owen Roe,
Of him who should have been thy King,
The noble Owen Roe

Alas, hapless land,
It is ever thus with thee ;
The eternal destinies withstand
Thy struggle to be free.
One after one thy champions fall,
Thy valiant men lie low,
And now sleeps under shroud and pall
The gallant Owen Roe,
The worthiest warrior of them all.
The princely Owen Roe!

Where was sword, where was soul
Like to his beneath the skies ?
Ah, many a century must roll
Ere such a chief shall rise!
I saw him in the battle's shock,
Tremendous was his blow,
As smites the sledge the anvil block
His blade smote the foe.
He was a tower; a human rock
Was mighty Owen Roe!

Woe to us! Guilt and wrong
Triumph, while to our grief
We raise the keen, the funeral song
Above our fallen chief.
The proud usurper sways with power,
He rules in state and show,
While we lament our fallen tower,
Our leader, Owen Roe;
While we, like slaves, bow down and cower,
And weep for Owen Roe.

But the high will of Heaven
Be fulfilled for evermore!
What tho'it leavest us bereaven
And stricken to the core.
Amid our groans, amid our tears,
We still feel and know
That we shall meet in after years
The sainted Owen Roe:
In after years, in brighter spheres,
Our glorious Owen Roe.

# THE RUINS OF DONEGAL CASTLE

*(From the Irish)*

O mournful, O forsaken pile,
What desolation dost thou dree!
How tarnished is the beauty that was thine erewhile,
Thou mansion of chaste melody!

Demolished lie thy towers and halls;
A dark, unsightly, earthen mound
Defaces the pure whiteness of thy shining walls,
And solitude doth gird thee round.

Fair fort! thine hour has come at length,
Thine older glory has gone by.
Lo! far beyond thy noble battlements of strength,
Thy corner-stones all scattered lie!

Where now, O rival of the gold
Emania, be thy wine-cups all?
Alas! for these thou now hast nothing but the cold,
Cold stream that from the heavens doth fall!

How often from thy turrets high,
Thy purple turrets, have we seen
Long lines of glittering ships, when summer-time drew nigh,
With masts and sails of snow-white sheen!

How often seen, when gazing round,
From thy tall towers, the hunting trains,
The blood-enlivening chase, the horseman hound,
Thou fastness of a hundred plains!

How often to thy banquets bright
We have seen the strong-armed Gaels repair,
And when the feast was over, once again unite
For battle, in thy bass-court fair!

Alas! for thee, thou fort forlorn !
Alas! for thy low, lost estate!
It is my woe of woes this melancholy morn,
To see thee left thus desolate!

Oh! there hath come of Connell's race
A many and many a gallant chief,
Who, if he saw thee now, thou of the once glad face
Could not dissemble his deep grief.

Could Manus of the lofty soul
Behold thee as this day thou art,
Thou of the regal towers! what bitter, bitter dole,
What agony would rend his heart!

He brought upon thee all this woe,
Thou of the fair-proportioned walls,
Lest thou shouldst ever yield a shelter to the foe,
Shouldst house the black, ferocious Galls!

Shouldst yet become in saddest truth
A *Dun-na*-Gall[1] - the strangers own.
For this cause only, stronghold of the Gaelic youth,
Lie thy majestic towers o'erthrown.

It is a drear, a dismal sight,
This of thy ruin and decay,
Now that our kings, and bards, and men of mark and might,
Are nameless exiles far away!

Yet, better thou shouldst fall, meseems,
By thine own king of many thrones,
Than that the truculent Galls should rear around thy streams
Dry mounds and circles of great stones.

As doth in many a desperate case
The surgeon by the malady,
So hath, O shield and bulwark of great Coffey's race,
Thy royal master done by thee!

[1] Fort of the Foreigner.

# A FAREWELL TO
# PATRICK SARSFIELD, EARL OF LUCAN[1]

*(From the Irish)*

Farewell, O Patrick Sarsfield, may luck be on your path!
    Your camp is broken up, your work is marred for years;
But you go to kindle into flame the King of France's wrath,
    Though you leave sick Eire in tears
                Och, ochone!

May the White sun and moon rain glory on your head,
    All hero as you are, and holy man of God!
To you the Saxons owe a many an hour of dread
    In the land you have often trod -
                Och, ochone!

The Son of Mary guard you, and bless you to the end!
    'Tis altered is the time when your legions were astir,
When at Cullen you were hailed as conqueror and friend,
    And you crossed Narrow-water, near Birr -
                Och, ochone!

I'll journey to the north, over mount, moor, and wave;
    'Twas there I first beheld drawn up, in file and line,
The brilliant Irish hosts; they were bravest of the brave,
    But, alas, they scorned to combine -
                Och, ochone!

I saw the royal Boyne when his billows flashed with blood;
    I fought at Graine Og, when a thousand horsemen fell ;
On the dark empurpled plain of Aughrim, too, I stood,
    On the plain by Tubberdonny's well -
                Och, ochone!

To the heroes of Limerick, the city of the fights,
    Be my best blessing borne on the wings of the air;
We had card-playing there o'er our camp fires at night,
    And the Word of Life, too, and prayer -
                Och, ochone!

But for you, Londonderry, may plague smite and slay
　　Your people, may ruin desolate you stone by stone!
Thro' you there's many a gallant youth lies coffinless to-day,
　　With the winds for mourners alone -
　　　　　　Och, ochone !

I clomb the high hill on a fair summer noon,
　　And saw the Saxons muster, clad in armour blinding bright;
Oh, rage withheld my hand, or gunsman and dragoon
　　Should have supped with Satan that night ! -
　　　　　　Och, ochone!

How many a noble soldier, how many a cavalier,
　　Careered along this road, seven fleeting weeks ago,
With silver~hilted sword, with matchlock and with spear,
　　Who now, mavrone! lies low -
　　　　　　Och, ochone !

All hail to thee, Ben Eder![2] I but ah, on thy brow
　　I see a limping soldier, who battled and who bled
Last year in the cause of the Stuart, though now
　　The worthy is begging his bread -
　　　　　　Och, ochone!

And Diarmid, O Diarmid! he perished in the strife;
　　His head it was spiked upon a halberd high;
His colours they were trampled: he had no chance of life
　　If the Lord God Himself stood by! -
　　　　　　Och, ochone!

But most, O my woe! I lament and lament
　　For the ten valiant heroes who dwelt nigh the Nore,
And my three blessed brothers; they left me and went
　　To the wars, and returned no more -
　　　　　　Och, ochone !

On the bridge of the Boyne was our first overthrow;
　　By Slavery the next, for we battled without rest;
The third was at Aughrim. O Eire! thy woe
　　Is a sword in my bleeding breast -
　　　　　　Och, ochone !

Oh, the roof above our heads, it was barbarously fired,
  While the black Orange guns blazed and bellowed around!
And as volley followed volley, Colonel Mitchel[3] inquired
  Whether Lucan still stood his ground? -
                Och, ochone !

But O'Kelly still remains, to defy and to toil,
  He has memories that hell won't permit him to forget,
And a sword that will make the blue blood flow like oil
  Upon many an Aughrim yet! -
                Och, ochone!

And I never shall believe that my fatherland can fall
  With the Burkes,[4] and the Decies, and the son of Royal James,[5]
And Talbot,[6] the captain, and Sarsfield above all,
  The beloved of damsels and dames
                Och, ochone!

[1] Sarsfield, one of the greatest of Irish heroes, left Ireland with the "wild geese," after the siege of Limerick, and fell at Landen in 1693.
[2] The Hill of Howth, near Dublin,
[3] John Michelbourne, Governor of Derry
[4] Such of the Burkes as were loyal to James.
[5] James Fitz-James, Duke of Berwick.
[6] Richard Talbot, Earl of Tryconnell.

# ROISIN DUBH¹

*(An Earlier Version of "Dark Rosaleen")*

Since last night's star, afar, afar,
Heaven saw my speed;
I seemed to fly o'er mountains high
On magic steed.
I dashed though Erne! The world may learn
The cause from love:
For light or sun shone on me none,
But Roisin Dubh !

O Roisin mine, droop not, nor pine;
Look not so dull!
The Pope from Rome shall send thee home
A pardon full;
The priests are near; O do not fear!
From heaven above
They come to thee, they come to free
My Roisin Dubh!

Thee have I loved, for thee have roved
O'er land and sea;
My heart was sore, and ever more
It beat for thee;
I could not weep, I could not sleep,
I could not move!
For night or day, I dreamed alway
Of Roisin Dubh !

Thro' Munster land, by shore and strand,
Far could I roam,
If I might get my loved one yet,
And bring her home.
O sweetest flower, that blooms in bower,
Or dell or grove!
Thou lovest me, and I love thee,
My Roisin Dubh !

The sea shall burn, the skies shall mourn,
The skies rain blood,
The world shall rise in dread surprise
And warful mood,
And hill and lake in Eire shake,
And hawk turn dove,
Ere you shall pine, ere you decline,
My Roisin Dubh !

¹The little black rose

# SOUL AND COUNTRY

Arise! my slumbering soul, arise!
And learn what yet remains for thee
To dree or do!
The signs are flaming in the skies;
A struggling world would yet be free,
And live anew.
The earthquake hath not yet been born,
That soon shall rock the lands around
Beneath their base.
Immortal freedom's thunder horn,
As yet, yields but a doleful sound
To Europe's race.

Look round, my soul and see and say
If those around thee understand
Their mission here;
The will to smite- the power to slay -
Abound in every heart and hand,
Afar, anear.
But, God! must yet the conqueror's sword
Pierce mind, as heart, in this proud year?
O, dream it not!
It sounds a false, blaspheming word,
Begot and born of mortal fear -
And ill begot!

To leave the world a name is nought;
To leave a name for glorious deeds
And works of love -
A name to waken lightning thought,
And fire the soul of him who reads
This tells above.
Napoleon sinks to-day before
The ungilded shrine, the single soul
Of Washington;
Truth's name, alone, shall man adore,
Long as the waves of time shall roll
Henceforward on!

My countrymen! my words are weak,
My health is gone my soul is dark,
My heart is chill-
Yet would I fain and fondly seek
To see you borne in freedoms bark
O'er ocean still.
Beseech your God, and bide your hour -
He cannot, will not, long be dumb;
Even now his tread
Is heard o'er earth with coming power ;
And coming, trust me it will come,
Else were He dead!

# A VISION OF CONNAUGHT IN THE
# THIRTEENTH CENTURY

I walked entranced
Through a land of Morn;
The sun, with wondrous excess of light,
Shone down and glanced
Over seas of corn
And lustrous gardens aleft and right.
Even in the clime
Of resplendent Spain,
Beams no such sun upon such a land;
But it was the time,
'Twas in the reign,
Of Cahal Mór of the Wine-red Hand.

Anon stood nigh
By my side a man
Of princely aspect and port sublime.
Him queried I
" O, my Lord and Khan,[1]
What clime is this, and what golden time?"
When he - "The clime
Is a clime to praise,
The clime is Erin's, the green and bland;
And it is the time,
These be the days,
Of Cahal Mór of the Wine-red Hand!"

Then saw I thrones,
And circling fires,
And a Dome rose near me, as by a spell,
Whence flowed the tones
Of silver lyres,
And many voices in wreathed swell;
And their thrilling chime
Fell on mine ears
As the heavenly hymn of an angel-band -
" It is now the time,
These be the years,
Of Cahal Mór of the Wine-red Hand! "

I sought the hall,
And, behold! - a change
From light to darkness, from joy to woe!
King, nobles, all,
Looked aghast and strange;
The minstrel-group sate in dumbest show!
Had some great crime
Wrought this dread amaze,
This terror?  None seemed to understand
'Twas then the time,
We were in the days,
Of Cahal Mór of the Wine-red Hand.

I again walked forth;
But lo! the sky
Showed fleckt with blood, and an alien sun
Glared from the north,
And there stood on high,
Amid his shorn beams, a skeleton!
It was by the stream
Of the castled Maine,
One Autumn eve, in the Teuton's land,
That I dreamed this dream
Of the time and reign
Of Cahal Mór of the Wine-red Hand!


[1] *Ceann*, the Gaelic title for a chief.

# THE WARNING VOICE[1]

Ye Faithful  -  ye noble!
A day is at hand
Of trial and trouble,
And woe in the land!
O'er a once greenest path,
Now blasted and sterile,
Its dusk shadows loom -
It cometh with Wrath,
With Conflict and Peril,
With Judgment and Doom!

False bands shall be broken,
Dead systems shall crumble,
And the haughty shall hear
Truths never yet spoken,
Though smouldering like flame
Through many a lost year
In the hearts of the Humble;
For hope will expire
As the terror draws nigher,
And, with it, the Shame
Which so long overawed
Men's minds by its might -
And the Powers abroad
Will be Panic and Blight,
And phrenetic Sorrow
Black Pest all the night,
And Death on the morrow!

Now, therefore, ye True,
Gird your loins up anew!
By the good you have wrought?
By all you have thought,
And suffered, and done!
By your souls! I implore you,
Be leal to your mission  -
Remembering that one
Of the two paths before you
Slopes down to Perdition!

To you have been given,
Not granaries and gold,
But the Love that lives long,
And waxes not cold;
And the Zeal that has striven
Against Error and Wrong,
And in fragments had riven
The chains of the strong!
Bide now, by your sternest
Conceptions of earnest
Endurance for others,
Your weaker-souled brothers!
Your true faith and worth
Will be History soon,
And their stature stand forth
In the unsparing Noon!
You have dreamed of an era
Of Knowledge, and truth,
And Peace -the true glory!
Was this a chimera?
Not so! - but the childhood and youth
Of our days will grow hoary,
Before such a marvel shall burst on their sight!
On you its beams glow not
For you its flowers blow not,
You cannot rejoice in its light,
But in darkness and suffering instead,
You go down to the place of the Dead!
To this generation
The sore tribulation,
The stormy commotion,
And foam of the Popular Ocean,
The struggle of class against class;
The Dearth and the Sadness,
The Sword and the War-vest;
To the next, the Repose and the Gladness,
" The Sea of clear glass,"
And the rich Golden Harvest.

58

Know, then, your true lot,
Ye faithful, though few!
Understand your position,
Remember your mission,
And vacillate not,
Whatsoever ensue!
Alter not! Falter not!
Palter not now with your own living souls,
When each moment that rolls
May see Death lay his hand
On some new victim's brow!
Oh! let not your vow
Have been written in sand!
Leave cold calculations,
Of Danger and Plague,
To the slaves and the traitors
Who cannot dissemble
The dastard sensations
That now make them tremble
With phantasies vague! -
The men without ruth -
The hypocrite haters
Of Goodness and Truth,
Who at heart curse the race
Of the sun through the skies;
And would look in God's face
With a lie in their eyes!
To the last do your duty,
Still mindful of this
That Virtue is Beauty,
And Wisdom, and Bliss;
So, howe'er, as frail men, you have erred on
Your way along Life's thronged road,
Shall your consciences prove a sure guerdon
And tower of defence,
Until Destiny summon you hence
To the Better Abode!

¹ Written in the year 1847, when the Famine was wasting Ireland.

# IRISH NATIONAL HYMN

O Ireland!   Ancient Ireland!
Ancient! yet for ever young!
Thou our mother, home and sire-land  -
Thou at length hast found a tongue  -
Proudly thou, at length,
Resistest in triumphant strength.
Thy flag of freedom floats unfurled;
And as that mighty God existeth,
Who giveth victory when and where He listeth,
Thou yet shalt wake and shake the nations of the world.

For this dull world still slumbers,
Weetless of its wants or loves,
Though, like Galileo, numbers
Cry aloud, "It moves! it moves!"
In a midnight dream,
Drifts it down Time's Wreckful stream -
All march, but few descry the goal.
0 Ireland! be it thy high duty
To teach the world the might of Moral Beauty,
And stamp God's image truly on the struggling soul.
Strong in thy self-reliance,
Not in idle threat or boast,
Hast thou hurled thy fierce defiance
At the haughty Saxon host,
Thou hast claimed, in sight
Of high Heaven, thy long-lost right.
Upon thy hills - along thy plains
In the green bosom of thy valleys,
The new-born soul of holy freedom rallies,
And calls on thee to trample down in dust thy chains!

Deep, saith the Eastern story,
Burns in Iran's mines a gem,
For its dazzling hues and glory
Worth a Sultan's diadem.
But from human eyes,
Hidden there it ever lies !

The aye-travailing Gnomes alone,
Who toil to form the mountain's treasure,
May gaze and gloat with pleasure, without measure,
Upon the lustrous beauty of that wonder-stone.
So is it with a nation,
Which would win for its rich dower
That bright pearl, Self-liberation -
It must labour hour by hour.


Strangers who travail
To lay bare the gem, shall fail;
Within itself must grow, must glow-
Within the depth of its own bosom,
Must flower in loving might, must broadly blossom,
The hopes that shall be born ere Freedom's Tree can blow
Go on, then, all rejoiceful !
March on thy career unbowed!
Ireland! let thy noble, voiceful
Spirit cry to God aloud!
Man will bid thee speed  -
God will aid thee in thy need  -
The Time, the Hour, the Power are near  -
Be sure thou soon shalt form the vanguard
Of that illustrious band, whom Heaven and Man guard:
And these words come from one whom some have called a Seer.

# TO MY NATIVE LAND

Awake! arise! shake off thy dreams!
Thou art not what thou wert of yore:
Of all those rich, those dazzling beams,
That once illum'd thine aspect o'er
Show me a solitary one
Whose glory is not quenched and gone.

The harp remaineth where it fell,
With mouldering frame and broken chord;
Around the song there hangs no spell
No laurel wreath entwines the sword;
And startlingly the footstep falls
Along thy dim and dreary halls.

When other men in future years,
In wonder ask, how this could be?
Then answer only by thy tears,
That ruin fell on thine and thee;
Because thyself wouldst have it so -
Because thou welcomedst the blow!

To stamp dishonour on thy brow
Was not within the power of earth;
And art thou agonised, when now
The hour that lost thee all thy worth,
And turned thee to the thing thou art,
Rushes upon thy bleeding heart?

Weep, weep, degraded one - the deed,
The desperate deed was all thine own:
Thou madest more than maniac speed
To hurl thine honours from their throne.
Thine honours fell, and when they fell
The nations rang thy funeral knell.

Well may thy sons be seared in soul,
Their groans be deep by night and day;
Till day and night forget to roll,
Their noblest hopes shall morn decay -
Their freshest flowers shall die by blight -
Their brightest sun shall set at night.

The stranger, as he treads thy sod,
And views thy universal wreck,
May execrate the foot that trod
Triumphant on a prostrate neck;
But what is that to thee? Thy woes
May hope in vain for pause or close.

Awake! arise! shake off thy dreams!
'Tis idle all to talk of power,
And fame and glory - these are themes
Befitting ill so dark an hour;
Till miracles be wrought for thee,
Nor fame nor glory shalt thou see.

Thou art forsaken by the earth,
Which makes a byword of thy name;
Nations, and thrones, and powers whose birth
As yet is not, shall rise to fame,
Shall flourish and may fall - but thou
Shalt linger as thou lingerest now.

And till all earthly power shall wane,
And Time's grey pillar, groaning, fall;
Thus shall it be, and still in vain
Thou shalt essay to burst the thrall
Which binds, in fetters forged by fate,
The wreck and ruin of what once was great.

# THE DYING ENTHUSIAST

Speak no more of life, what can life bestow,
In this amphitheatre of strife,
All times dark with tragedy and woe?
Knowest thou not how care and pain
Build their lampless dwellings in the brain,
Ever, as the stern intrusion
Of our teachers, time and truth,
Turn to gloom the bright illusion,
Rainbowed on the soul of youth?
Could I live to find that this is so?
Oh! no! no!

As the stream of time sluggishly doth flow,
Look how all beaming and sublime,
Sinks into the black abysm below
Yea, the loftiest intelllect,
Earliest on the strand of life is wrecked.
Nought of lovely, nothing glorious,
Lives to triumph o'er decay ;
Desolation reigns victorious-
Mind in dungeon-walled by clay ;
Could I bear to feel mine own laid low?
Oh! no! no!

Restless o'er the earth thronging millions go:
But behold how genius, love, and worth,
Move like lonely phantoms to and fro.
Suns are quenched, and kingdoms fall,
But the doom of these outdarkens all!
Die they then? Yes, love's devotion,
Stricken, withers in its bloom ;
Fond affections, deep as ocean,
In their cradle find their tomb :
Shall I linger, then, to count each throe?
Oh! no! no!

Prison-bursting death! welcome be thy blow!
Thine is but the forfeit of my breath,
Not the spirit! nor the spirit's glow.
Spheres of beauty-hallowed spheres,
Undefaced by time, undimmed by tears,
Henceforth hail! oh, who would grovel,
In a world impure as this?
Who would weep, in cell or hovel,
When a palace might be his?
Wouldst thou have me the bright lot forego?
Oh! no! no!

# LINES ON THE DEATH OF A
# BELOVED FRIEND

I stood aloof: I dared not to behold
Thy relics covered over with the mould;
I shed no tear  -  I uttered not a groan,
But oh! I felt heart-broken and alone!

How feel I now? The bitterness of grief
Has passed, for all that is intense is brief  -
A softer sadness overshades my mind,
But there thine image ever lies enshrined.

And if I mourn  -  for this is human, too  -
I mourn no longer that thy days were few,
Nor that thou hast escaped the tears and woe,
And deaths on deaths the Living undergo.

Thou fadedst in the Spring  -  time of thine years  -
Life's juggling joys and spirit  -  wasting fears
Thou knewest but in romance  -  and to thine eyes
Man shone a god  -  the earth a Paradise!

Thou diedst ere the icy breath of Scorn
Froze the warm feelings of thy girlhood's morn  -
Ere thou couldst learn that Man is but a slave,
And this blank world a prison and a grave.

Thy spirit is at peace  -  Peace! blessed word!
Forgotten by the million  -  or unheard;
But mine still struggles down this Vale of Death,
And courts the favour of a little breath!

Through every stage of Life's consuming fever
The soul too often is her own deceiver,
And revels  -  even in a world like this
In golden visions of unbounded bliss.

But he who, looking on the naked chart
Of Life, feels nature sinking at his heart,
He who is drugged with sorrows, he for whom
Affliction carves a pathway to the tomb,

He will unite - with me to bless that Power
Who gathers and transplants the fragile flower
Ere yet the spirit of the whirlwind storm
Comes forth in wrath to prostrate and deform.

And if it be that God Himself removes
From peril and contagion those He loves,
Weep such no more - but strew with freshest roses
The hallowed mound where Innocence reposes.

So may bright lilies and each odorous flower
Grow o'er thy grave and form a beauteous bower,
Exhaust their sweetness on the gales around,
And drop, for grief, their honey on the ground!

The world is round me now, but sad and single
I stand amid the throng with whom I mingle;
Not one of all of whom can be to me
The bosom treasure I have lost in thee.

# TWENTY GOLDEN YEARS AGO

O, the rain, the weary, dreary rain,
How it splashes on the window-sill!
Night, I guess too, must be on the wane,
Strass and Gass¹ around are grown so still.
Here I sit, with coffee in my cup -
Ah! 'twas rarely I beheld it flow
In the taverns where I loved to sup
Twenty golden years ago!

Twenty years ago, alas! - but stay,
On my life, 'tis half-past twelve o'clock!
After all, the hours do slip away-
Come, here goes to burn another block!
For the night, or morn, is wet and cold,
And my fire is dwindling rather low :
I had fire enough, when young and bold,
Twenty golden years ago!

Dear! I don't feel well at all, somehow:
Few in Weimar dream how bad I am;
Floods of tears grow common with me now,
High-Dutch floods, that Reason cannot dam.
Doctors think I'll neither live nor thrive
If I mope at home so  -  I don't know
Am I living now? I was alive
Twenty golden years ago.

Wifeless, friendless, flagonless, alone,
Not quite bookless, though, unless I chuse,
Left with nought to do, except to groan,
Not a soul to woo, except the Muse  -
O! this, this is hard for me to bear,
Me, who whilome lived so much en haut,
Me, who broke all hearts like chinaware
Twenty golden years ago!

68

P'rhaps 'tis better:- Time's defacing waves
Long have quenched the radiance of my brow -
They who curse me nightly from their graves
Scarce could love me were they living now;
But my loneliness hath darker ills -
Such dun-duns as Conscience, Thought and Co.,
Awful Gorgons! worse than tailors' bills
Twenty golden years ago!

Did I paint a fifth of what I feel,
O, how plaintive you would ween I was!
But I won't, albeit I have a deal
More to wail about than Kerner has!
Kerner's tears are wept for withered flowers,
Mine for withered hopes; my Scroll of Woe
Dates, alas! from Youth's deserted bowers,
Twenty golden years ago!

Yet may Deutschland's bardlings flourish long!
Me, I tweak no beak among them;- hawks
Must not pounce on hawks; besides, in song
I could once beat all of them by chalks.
Though you find me, as I near my goal,
Sentimentalising like Rousseau,
O! I had a grand Byronian soul
Twenty golden years ago!

Tick-tick, tick-tick! - Not a sound save Time's,
And the windgust, as it drives the rain
Tortured torturer of reluctant rhymes,
Go to bed, and rest thine aching brain!
Sleep! - no more the dupe of hopes or schemes;
Soon thou sleepest where the thistles blow-
Curious anticlimax to thy dreams
Twenty golden years ago!

¹ Street and lane.

# THE COMING EVENT

Curtain the lamp, and bury the bowl -
The ban is on drinking!
Reason shall reign the queen of the soul
When the spirits are sinking.
Chained lies the demon that smote with blight
Men's morals and laurels;
So, hail to Health, and a long Good-night
To old wine and new quarrels!

Nights shall descend, and no taverns ring
To the roar of our revels;
Mornings shall dawn, but none of them bring
White lips and blue devils.
Riot and Frenzy sleep with Remorse
In the obsolete potion,
And Mind grows calm as a ship on her course
O'er the level of Ocean.

So should it be! - for Man's world of romance
Is fast disappearing,
And shadows of CHANGES are seen in advance,
Whose epochs are nearing;
And days are at hand when the Best will require
All means of salvation,
And the souls of men shall be tried in the fire
Of the Final Probation.

And the Witling no longer or sneers or smiles;
And the Worldling dissembles;
And the blank-minded Sceptic feels anxious at whiles,
And wonders and trembles;
And fear and defiance are blent in the jest
Of the blind Self-deceiver;
And infinite hope is born in the breast
Of the childlike Believer.

Darken the lamp, then, and bury the bowl,
Ye Faithfullest-hearted!
And, as your swift years hasten on to the goal
Whither worlds have departed,
Spend all, sinew, soul, in your zeal to atone
For the past and its errors;
So best shall ye bear to encounter alone
THE EVENT and its terrors.

# COUNSEL TO THE WORLDLY-WISE

Go A-Foot and go A-head!
That's the way to prosper;
Whoso must be carriage-led
Suffereth serious loss per
Day in health as well as wealth,
By that laziness with which
Walkers have from birth warred;
And ere long grim Death by stealth
Mounts the tilbury, and the rich
Loller tumbleth earthward!

Also keep your conscience pure-
Neither lie nor borrow;
He who starves to-day, be sure
Always carves to-morrow.
March in front; don't sulk behind;
Dare to live, though sneering groups
Dub you rara avis -
"Serve your country-love your kind,"
And whene'er your spirit droops,
Think of Thomas Davis! [1]

[1] This is the only tribute paid by Mangan to one of the noblest of
Irish patriots and poets.

## COUNSEL OF A COSMOPOLITAN

Give smiles and sighs alike to all,
Serve all, but love not any;
Love's dangerous and delicious thrall
Hath been the tomb of many.

The sweetest wine-thoughts of the heart
Are turned ere long to bitter;
Sad memories loom when joys depart,
And gloom comes after glitter.

Why pawn thy soul for one lone flower,
And slight the whole bright garland;
Clarissa's eyes, Lucinda's bower,
Will fail thee in a far land!

Love God and Virtue! Love the Sun,
The Stars, the Trees, the Mountains!
The only living streams that run
Flow from Eternal Fountains!

# REST ONLY IN THE GRAVE

I rode till I reached the House of Wealth -
Twas filled with Riot and blighted health.

I rode till I reached the House of Love -
Twas vocal with sighs beneath and above!

I rode till I reached the House of Sin -
There were shrieks and curses without and within.

I rode till I reached the House of Toil -
Its inmates had nothing to bake or boil.

I rode in search of the House of Content
But could never reach it, far as I went!

The House of Quiet, for strong and weak
And Poor and rich, I have still to seek -

That House is narrow, and dark, and small -
But the only Peaceful House of all!

# THE NIGHT IS FALLING

The night is falling in chill December,
The frost is mantling the silent stream,
Dark mists are shrouding the mountain's brow;
My soul is weary: I now
Remember
The days of roses but as a dream.

The icy hand of the old Benumber,
The hand of Winter is on my brain,
I try to smile, while I inly grieve;
I dare not hope or believe
That Summer
Will ever brighten the earth again.

So, gazing grave wards, albeit immortal,
Man cannot pierce through the girdling Night
That sunders Time from Eternity,
Nor feel this death-vale to be
The portal
To realms of glory and Living Light

# THE GERALDINE'S DAUGHTER

*(From the Irish of Egan O'Rahilly.)*

A beauty all stainless, a pearl of a maiden,
Has plunged me in trouble and wounded my heart;
With sorrow and gloom is my soul overladen,
An anguish is there that will never depart.
I would voyage to Egypt, across the deep water,
Nor care about bidding dear Eire farewell,
So I only might gaze on the Geraldine's daughter
And sit by her side in some, green pleasant dell!

Her curling locks wave round her figure of lightness,
All dazzling and long, like the purest of gold;
Her blue eyes resemble twin stars in their brightness,
And her brow is like marble or wax to behold.
The radiance of heaven illumines her features
Where the snows and the rose have erected their throne;
It would seem that the sun had forgotten all creatures,
To shine on the Geraldine's daughter alone.

Her bosom is swan-white, her waist smooth and slender;
Her speech is like music, so sweet and so fair;
The feelings that glow in her noble heart lend her
A mien and a majesty lovely to see.
Her lips, red as berries, but riper than any,
Would kiss away even a sorrow like mine!
No wonder such heroes and noblemen many
Should cross the blue ocean to kneel at her shrine.

She is sprung from the Geraldine race, the great Grecians,
Niece of Mileadh's sons of the Valorous Bands,
Those heroes, the seed of the olden Phoenicians,
Though now trodden down, without fame, without lands;
Of her ancestors flourished the Barrys and Powers,
To the Lords of Bunratty she, too is allied,
And not a proud noble near Cashel's high towers
But is kin to this maiden the Geraldine's pride.

Of Saxon or Gael there is none to excel in
Her wisdom, her features, her figure, this fair;
In all she surpasses the far-famed Helen,
Whose beauty drove thousands to death and despair.
Whoe'er could but gaze on her aspect so noble
Would feel from thenceforward all anguish depart;
Yet for me tis, alas! my worst woe and my trouble
That her image must always abide in my heart

# THE SONG OF GLADNESS

*(From the Irish of William Heffernan)*

It was on a balmy evening, as June was departing fast,
That alone, and meditating in grief on the times a-past,
I wandered through the gloomsome shades
Of bosky Aherlow,
A wilderness of glens and glades,
When suddenly a thrilling strain of song
Broke forth upon the air in one incessant flow;
Sweeter it seemed to me (both voice and word)
Than harmony of the harp, or carol of the bird,
For it foretold fair Freedom's triumph, and the doom of Wrong.

The celestial hymns and anthems, that far o'er the sounding sea
Come to Erin from the temples of bright-bosomed Italy;
The music which from hill and rath
The playful fairy race
Pour on the wandering warrior's path,
Bewildering him with wonder and delight,
Or the cuckoo's full note from some green sunless place,
Some sunken thicket in a stilly wood,
Had less than that rich melody made mine Irish blood
Bound in its veins for ecstasy, or given my soul new might!

And while as I stood I listened, behold, thousand swarm of bees,
All arrayed in gay gold armour, shone red through the dusky trees;
I felt a boding in my soul,
A truthful boding, too,
That Erin's days of gloom and dole
Will soon be but remembered as a dream,
And the olden glory show eclipsed by the new.
Where the Usurper[1] then be?  Banished far!
Where his vile hireling henchmen?  Slaughtered all in war!
For blood shall rill down every hill, and blacken every stream.

I am Heffernan of Shronehill: my land mourns in thraldom long;
And I see but one sad sight here, the weak trampled bythe strong,
Yet if to-morrow underneath
A burial-stone I lay,
Clasped in the skeleton arms of death,
And if a pilgrim wind again should waft
Over my noteless grave the song I heard to-day,
I would spring up revivified, reborn,
A living soul again, as on my birthday morn,
Ay! even though coffined, over-earthed, tombed-in, and epitaphed!

[1.] George I.

# THE FAIR HILLS OF EIRE, O!

*(From the Irish of Donogh Mac-Con-Mara, or MacNamara)*

Take a blessing from my heart to the land of my birth,
 And the fair hills of Eire, O!
And to all that yet survive of Eibhear's tribe on earth,
 On the fair hills of Eire, O!
In that land so delightful the wild thrush's lay
Seems to pour a lament forth for Eire's decay.
Alas, alas! why pine I a thousand miles away
 From the fair hills of Eire, O!


The soil is rich and soft, the air is mild and bland,
 On the fair hills of Eire, O!
Her barest rock is greener to me than this rude land;
 O, the fair hills of Eire, O!
Her woods are tall and straight, grove rising over grove,
Trees flourish in her glens below and on her heights above;
Ah! in heart and in soul I shall ever, ever love
 The fair hills of Eire, O!


A noble tribe, moreover, are the now hapless Gael,
 On the fair hills of Eire, O!
A tribe in battle's hour unused to shrink or fail,
 On the fair hills of Eire, O!
For this is my lament in bitterness outpoured
To see them slain or scattered by the Saxon sword;
O, woe of woes! to see a foreign spoiler horde
 On the fair hills of Eire, O!

Broad and tall rise the cruachs in the golden morning glow
On the fair hills of Eire, O!
O'er her smooth grass for ever, sweet cream and honey flow
On the fair hills of Eire, O!
Oh, I long, I am pining, again to behold
The land that belongs to the brave Gael of old!
Far dearer to my heart than a gift of gems or gold
Are the fair hills of Eire, O!


The dewdrops lie bright 'mid the grass and yellow corn
On the fair hills of Eire, O!
The sweet-scented apples blush redly in the morn
On the fair hills of Eire, O!
The water-cress and sorrel fill the vales below,
The streamlets are hushed till the evening breezes blow,
While the waves of the Suir, noble river! eyer flow
'Neath the fair hills of Eire, O!


A fruitful clime is Eire, through valley, meadow, plain,
And the fair hills of Eire, O!
The very bread of life is in the yellow grain
On the fair hills of Eire, O!
Far dearer unto me than the tones music yields
Is the lowing of the kine and the calves in her fields,
In the sunlight that shone long ago on the shields
Of the Gaels, on the fair hills of Eire, O!

# OWEN REILLY: A KEEN

*(From the Irish)*

### I.

Oh! lay aside the flax, and put away the wheel,
And sing with me, but not in gladness
The heart that's in my breast is like to break with sadness -
God, God alone knows what I feel!

### 11

There's a lone, a vacant place beside the cheerless hearth,
A spot my eyes are straining after
Oh! never more from thence will ring my boy's light laughter,
The outgushing of his young heart's mirth!

### III.

No more will his hands clasp the cross before the shrine
Of Christ's immaculate Virgin Mother.
Never, oh! never more will he pour forth another
Prayer for himself, or me, or mine!

### IV.

The young men on the mountain sides will miss - miss long,
The fleetest hurler of their number.
Powerless, alas! to-night in death's unbroken slumber,
Lies he, the Lithe of Limb, the Strong!

### V.

Oh! raise the keen, young women, o'er my darling's grave -
Oh! kneel in prayer o'er his low dwelling;
At break of day this morn there knelt his mother, telling
Her beads for him she could not save!

### VI.

Oh! plant, young men, the Shamrock near my darling's head,
And raise the hardy fir tree over
The spot : the strange wayfarer then will know they cover
My Oweneen's dark burial-bed!

### VII.

Heard ye not, yestereven, the Banshee deplore
His death on heath-clad Killenvallen?
"Ul-ullalu! " she cried, "a green young oak is fallen,
For Owen Reilly lives no more!"

### VIII

There stands a lone grey hazel-tree in Glen-na-ree,
Whose green leaves put buds forth and wither.
I sigh and groan as often as I wander thither,
For I am like that lone grey tree!

### IX.

My four beloved sons, where are they? Have they not
Left me a wreck here all as lonely?
They withered and they died! I, their old mother, only
Remain to weep and wail my lot!

### X.

But I will follow them now soon; for oft amid
The storm I hear their voices calling,
"Come home!" - and in my dreams I see the cold clay falling
Heavily on my coffin-lid!

### XI.

When the dark night films o'er my eyes, oh! let me be
Laid out by Aileen Bawn Devany;
And let the lights around me at my wake be as many
As the white hairs yet left to me!

## XII.

See that the tall white slender gowans blow and bloom
In the grass round my head-stone brightly;
I would not have the little orphan daisy nightly
Mourning in solitude and gloom!

## XIII.

Let there be shrieking on the hill and in the glen,
Throughout the length and breadth of Galway's
Green land! Kathleen Dubh Reilly has herself been always
The Queen of Keeners; mourn her then!

## XIV.

Lights will be seen to dance along Carn Corra's height,
And through the burial-field; but follow
Them not, young men and women! for, o'er hill and hollow
They will but lure to Death and Night!

## XV.

But come ye to my grave when, in the days of May,
The gladsome sun and skies grow warmer,
And say, "Here sleeps Kathleen, where tempest cannot harm her,
Soft be her narrow bed of clay!"

## XVI.

And count your beads, and pray, "Rest her poor soul, O God!
She willed no ill to breathing mortal
Grant her, then, Thou, a place within Heaven's blessed portal,
Now that her bones lie in the sod!"

# WELCOME TO THE PRINCE OF OSSORY

*(From the Irish of William Heffernan the Blind)*

### I.

Lift . . . up the drooping head,
Meehal Dubh Mac-Giolla-Kierin!
Her blood yet boundeth red
Through the myriad veins of Erin.
No! no! she is not dead,
Meehal Dubh Mac-Giolla-Kierin!
Lo! she redeems
The lost years of bygone ages
New glory beams
Henceforth on her History's pages!
Her long penitential Night of Sorrow
Yields at length before the reddening Morrow!

### II

You . . . heard the thunder-shout,
Meehal Dubh Mac-Giolla-Kierin!
Saw lightning streaming out
O'er the purple hills of Erin!
And bide you yet in doubt,
Meehal Dubh Mac-Goilla-Kierin?
O! doubt no more!
Through Ulidia's voiceful valleys,
On ...Shannon's shore,
Freedom's burning spirit rallies,
Earth and Heaven unite in sign and omen[1]
Bodeful of the downfall of our foemen.

### III

Thurot commands the North,
Meehal Dubh Mac-Giolla-Kierin!
Louth sends her heroes forth
To hew down the foes of Erin!
Swords gleam in field and gorth,
Up! up! my friend!
There's a glorious goal before us;
Here will we blend

Speech and soul in this grand chorus -
"By the Heaven that gives us one more token,
We will die, or see our shackles broken!"

IV

Charles[2] leaves the Grampian hills,
Meehal Dubh Mac-Giolla-Kierin!
Charles, whose appeal yet thrills,
Like a clarion-blast, through Erin
Charles, he whose image fills
Thy soul, too, Mac-Giolla-Kierin!
Ten . . . thousand strong,
His clans move in brilliant order,
Sure that e'er long
He will march them o'er the Border,
While the dark-haired daughters of the Highlands
Crown with wreaths the Monarch of three islands!

V

Fill, then, the ale-cup high,
Meehal Dubh Mac-Giolla-Kierin!
Fill! - the bright hour is nigh
That shall give her own to Erin!
Those who so sadly sigh,
Even as you, Mac-Giolla-Kierin,
Henceforth shall sing.
Hark! - O'er heathery hill and dell come
Shouts for the King!
Welcome, our Deliverer! Welcome!
Thousands this glad night, ere turning bedward,
Will, with us, drink "Victory to Charles Edward!"

[1] An allusion to that well-known atmospherical phenomenon of the "cloud-armies," which is said to have been so common about this period (1745), in Scotland.

[2] Charles Stuart

# LAMENTATION OF MAC LIAG FOR KINCORA[1]

*(From the Irish)*

Oh, where, Kincora! is Brian the Great?
And where is the beauty that once was thine?
Oh, where are the princes and nobles that sate
At the feast in thy halls, and drank the red wine?
Where, oh, Kincora?

Oh, where, Kincora! are thy valorous lords?
Oh, whither, thou Hospitable! are they gone?
Oh, where are the Dalcassians of the Golden Swords? [2]
And where are the warriors Brian led on?
Where, oh, Kincora?

And where is Murrough, the descendant of kings -
The defeater of a hundred - the daringly brave -
Who set but slight store by jewels and rings -
Who swam down the torrent and laughed at its wave?
Where, oh, Kincora?

And where is Donogh, King Brian's worthy son?
And where is Conaing, the Beautiful Chief?
And Kian, and Corc? Alas! they are gone -
They have left me this night alone with my grief!
Left me, Kincora!

And where are the chiefs with whom Brian went forth,
The ne'er-vanquished son of Evin the Brave,
The great King of Onaght, renowned for his worth,
And the hosts of Baskinn, from the western wave?
Where, oh, Kincora?

Oh, where is Duvlann of the Swift-footed Steeds?
And where is Kian, who was son of Molloy?
And where is King Lonergan, the fame of whose deeds
In the red battle-field no time can destroy?
Where, oh, Kincora?

And where is that youth of majestic height,
The faith-keeping Prince of the Scots ? - Even he,
As wide as his fame was, as great as was his might,
Was tributary, oh, Kincora, to thee!
                    Thee, oh, Kincora!

They are gone, those heroes of royal birth,
Who plundered no churches, and broke no trust,
Tis weary for me to be living on earth
When they, oh, Kincora, lie low in the dust!
                    Low, oh, Kincora!

Oh, never again will Princes appear,
To rival the Dalcassians of the Cleaving Swords!
I can never dream of meeting afar or anear,
In the east or the west, such heroes and lords!
                    Never, Kincora!

Oh, dear are the images my memory calls up
Of Brian Boru! - how he never would miss
To give me at the banquet the first bright cup!
Ah! why did he heap on me honour like this?
                    Why, oh, Kincora?

I am Mac Liag, and my home is on the Lake;
Thither often, to that palace whose beauty is fled,
Came Brian to ask me, and I went for his sake.
Oh, my grief! that I should live, and Brian be dead!
                    Dead, oh, Kincora!

[1] Mac Liag was the secretary of Brian Boroihme, and wrote numerous poems.
He died in 1015.

Brian Boroihme is better known to us as Brian Boru.

[2] Coolg n-or, of the swords of gold, i.e., of the gold-hilted swords.

# A LULLABY

*(From the Irish of Owen Roe O'Sullivan)*

O, Hushaby, baby! why weepest thou?
The diadem yet shall adorn thy brow,
And the jewels thy sires had, long agone,
In the regal ages of Eoghan and Conn,
Shall all be thine.
O, hushaby, hushaby, child of mine!
My sorrow, my woe, to see thy tears,
Pierce into my heart like spears.


I'll give thee that glorious apple of gold
The three fair goddesses sought of old,
I'll give thee the diamond sceptre of Pan,
And the rod with which Moses, that holiest man,
Wrought marvels divine;
O, hushaby, hushaby, child of mine!


I'll give thee that courser, fleet on the plains,
That courser with golden saddle and reins,
Which Falvey rode, the mariner-lord,
When the blood of the Danes, at Cashel-na-Nord,
Flowed like to dark wine;
O, hushaby, hushaby, child of mine!


I'll give thee the dazzling sword was worn
By Brian on Cluan-tarava's[1] morn,
And the bow of Murrough, whose shaft shot gleams
That lightened as when the arrowy beams
Of the noon-sun shine;
O, hushaby, hushaby, child of mine!

And the hound that was wont to speed amain
From Cashel's rock to Bunratty's plain,
And the eagle from gloomy Aherlow,
And the hawl of Skellig; all these I bestow
On thee and thy line;
O, hushaby, hushaby, child of mine!


And the golden fleece that Jason bore
To Hellas' hero-peopled shore,
And the steel that Cuchullin bought of yore,
With cloak, and necklet, and golden store,
And meadows and kine ;
O, hushaby, hushaby, child of mine!


And Conal's unpierceable shirt of mail,
And the shield of Nish, the prince of the Gael,
These twain for thee, my babe, shall I win,
With the flashing spears of Achilles and Finn,
Each high as a pine;
O, hushaby, hushaby, child of mine!


And the swords of Diarmid and fierce Fingal,
The slayers on heath and (alas!) in hall ;
And the charmed helmet that Oscar wore
When he left MacTreoin to welter in gore,
Subdued and supine;
O, hushaby, hushaby, child of mine!


And the jewel wherewith Queen Eofa proved
The value and faith of the hero she loved;
The magic jewel that nerved his arm
To work his enemies deadly harm
On plain and on brine;
O, hushaby, hushaby, child of mine!

And the wondrous cloak renowned in song
The enchanted cloak of the dark Dubhlong,
By whose powerful aid he battled mid
The thick of his foes, unseen and hid,
This, too, shall be thine;
O, hushaby, hushaby, child of mine!


The last, not least, of thy weapons, my son,
Shall be the glittering glaive of O'Dunn,
The gift from AEnghus' powerful hands,
The hewer-down of the Fenian bands,
With edge so fine!
O, hushaby, hushaby, child of mine [1]


Even Hebe, who fills the nectar up
For Love, in his luminous crystal cup,
Shall pour thee out a wine in thy dreams,
As bright as thy poet-father's themes
When inspired by the wine;
O, hushaby, hushaby, child of mine!


And silken robes, and sweet, soft cates
Shalt thou wear, and eat beyond thy mates -
Ah, see, here comes thy mother Moirin!
She, too, has the soul of an Irish queen:
She scorns to repine!
Then, hushaby, hushaby, child of mine!
My sorrow, my woe, to see thy tears,
Pierce into my heart like spears.


[1] Clontarf.

# PRINCE ALFRID'S ITINERARY
# THROUGH IRELAND

*(From the Irish)*

I found in Innisfail the fair,
In Ireland while in exile there,
Women of worth, both grave and gay men,
Many clerics and many laymen.

I travelled its fruitful provinces round,
And in every one of the five I found,
Alike in church and in palace hall,
Abundant apparel and food for all.

Gold and silver I found, and money,
Plenty of wheat and plenty of honey ;
I found God's people rich in pity,
Found many a feast and many a city.

I also found in Armagh the splendid,
Meekness, wisdom, and prudence blended,
Fasting as Christ hath recommended,
And noble councillors untranscended.

I found in each great church moreo'er,
Whether on island or on shore,
Piety, learning, fond affection,
Holy welcome and kind protection.

I found the good lay monks and brothers
Ever beseeching help for others,
And in keeping the holy word
Pure as it came from Jesus the Lord.

I found in Munster unfettered of any,
Kings, and queens, and poets a many-
Poets well skilled in music and measure,
Prosperous doings, mirth and pleasure.

I found in Connaught the just, redundance
Of riches, milk in lavish abundance,
Hospitality, vigour, fame,
In Cruachan's land of heroic name.

I found in the country of Connall the glorious,
Bravest heroes, ever victorious ;
Fair-complexioned men and warlike,
Ireland's lights, the high, and starlike !

I found in Ulster, from hill and glen,
Hardy warriors, resolute men ;
Beauty that bloomed when youth was gone,
And strength transmitted from sire to son.

I found the noble district of Boyle,
*(next line illegible)*
Brehons, Erenachs, weapons bright
And horsemen bold and sudden in fight.

I found in Leinster the smooth and sleek,
From Dublin to Slewmargy's peak ;
Flourishing pastures, valour, health,
Long-living worthies, commerce, wealth.

I found besides, from Ara to Glea,
In the broad rich country of Ossorie,
Sweet fruits, good laws for all and each,
Great chess-players, men of truthful speech.

I found in Meath's fair principality,
Virtue, vigour, and hospitality ;
Candour, joyfulness, bravery, purity,
Ireland's bulwark and security.

I found strict morals in age and youth,
I found historians recording truth ;
The things I sing of in verse unsmooth,
I found them all- I have written sooth

Alfrid was later King of the Northumbrian Saxons. He was educated there in about the year 684. The original poem in Irish is attributed to Alfrid. The five provinces refer to the two Meaths which at that time formed a distinct province. Cruchan or Croghan was the name of the royal palace of Connaught.

*Brehon* = a law judge. *Erenach* = a ruler, an archdeacon.
*Slewmargy* = a mountain in Queens County, near the river Barrow.

# ELLEN BAWN

*(From the Irish)*

Ellen Bawn, O Ellen Bawn, you darling, darling dear, you,
Sit awhile beside me here, I'll die unless I'm near you!
'Tis for you I'd swim the Suir and breast the Shannon's Waters;
For, Ellen dear, you've not your peer in Galway's blooming daughters!

Had I Limerick's gems and gold at will to mete and measure,
Were Loughrea's abundance mine, and all Portumna's treasure,
These might lure me, might insure me many and many a new love,
But O! no bribe could pay your tribe for one like you, my true love!

Blessings be on Connaught! that's the place for sport and raking!
Blessing, too, my love, on you, a-sleeping and a-waking !
I'd have met you, dearest Ellen, when the sun went under,
But, woe! the flooding Shannon broke across my path in thunder!

Ellen! I'd give all the deer in Limerick's parks and arbours,
Ay, and all the ships that rode last year in Munster's harbours,
Could I blot from Time the hour I first became your lover,
For, O! you've given my heart a wound it never can recover!

Would to God that in the sod my corpse to-night were lying,
And the wild birds wheeling o'er it, and the winds a-sighing,
Since your cruel mother and your kindred choose to sever
Two hearts that Love would blend in one for ever and for ever!

# RURY AND DARVORGILLIA

Know ye the tale of the Prince of Oriel,
Of Rury, last of his line of kings?
I pen it here as a sad memorial
Of how much woe reckless folly brings,

Of a time that Rury rode woodwards, clothed
In silk and gold, on a hunting chase
He thought like thunder[1] on his betrothed,
And with clinched hand he smote his face.

"*Fareer!*[2] *Mabhron!*[3] Princess Darvorgilla!
Forgive she will not a slight like this;
But could she, dared she, I should be still a
Base wretch to wed her for heaven's best bliss.

" *Fareer! Fareer!* Princess Darvorgilla !
She has four hundred young bowmen bold;
But I - I love her, and would not spill a
Drop of their blood for ten torques[4] of gold.

"Still, woe to all who provoke to slaughter!
I count as nought, weighed with fame like mine,
The birth and beauty of Cairtre's daughter;
So, judge the sword between line and line!

"Thou, therefore, Calbhach,[5] go call a muster,
And wind the bugle by fort and dun!
When stains shall tarnish our house's lustre,
Then sets in darkness the noonday sun!"

But Calbhach answered- "Light need to do so!
Behold the noblest of heroes here!
What foe confronts us, I reck not whoso,
Shall flee before us like hunted deer!"

Spake Rury then - "Calbhach, as thou willest!
But see, old man, there be brief delay
For this chill parle is of all things chillest,
And my fleet courser must now away!

"Yet though thou march with thy legions townwards,
Well armed for ambush or treacherous fray,
Still see they point their bare weapons downwards,
As those of warriors averse to slay!"

Now, when the clansmen were armed and mounted,
The aged Calbhach gave way to fears;
For, foot and horsemen, they barely counted
A hundred cross-bows and forty spears.

And thus exclaimed he - " My soul is shaken!
We die the death, not of men, but slaves;
We sleep the sleep from which none awaken,
And scorn shall point at our tombless graves!"

Then out spake Fergal - "A charge so weighty
As this, O Rury, thou shouldst not throw
On a drivelling dotard of eight-and-eighty,
Whose arm is nerveless for spear or bow!"

But Rury answered - "Away! To-morrow
Myself will stand in Traghvally[(6)] town;
But, come what may come, this day I borrow
To hunt through Glafna the brown deer down!"

So, through the night, unto grey Traghvally,
The feeble Ceann led his hosts along;
But faint and heart-sore, they could not rally,
So deeply Rury had wrought them wrong.

Now, when the Princess beheld advancing
Her lover's troops with their arms reversed
In lieu of broadswords and chargers prancing,
She felt her heart's hopes were dead and hearsed.

And on her knees to her ireful father
She prayed - "O father, let this pass by;
War not against the brave Rury! Rather
Pierce this fond bosom and let me die!"

But Cairtre rose in volcanic fury,
And so he spake - "By the might of God,
I hold no terms with this craven Rury
Till he or I lie below the sod!

"Thou shameless child! Thou, alike unworthy
Of him, thy father, who speaks thee thus,
And her, my Mhearb,[7] who in sorrow bore thee,
Wilt thou dishonour thyself and us ?

"Behold! I march with my serried bowmen -
Four hundred thine and a thousand mine;
I march to crush these degraded foemen,
Who gorge the ravens ere day decline!"

Meet now both armies in mortal struggle,
The spears are shivered, the javelins fly;
But what strange terror, what mental juggle,
Be those that speak out of Calbhach's eye?

It is - it must be, some spell Satanic,
That masters him and his gallant host.
Woe, woe the day! An inglorious panic
O'erpowers the legions - and all is lost!

Woe, woe that day, and that hour of carnage!
Too well they witness to Fergal's truth!
Too well in bloodiest appeal they warn Age
Not lightly thus to match swords with Youth!

When Rury reached, in the red of morning,
The battle-ground, it was he who felt
The dreadful weight of this ghastly warning,
And what a blow had o'ernight been dealt!

So, glancing round him, and sadly groaning,
He pierced his breast with his noble blade;
Thus all too mournfully mis-atoning
For that black ruin his word had made.

But hear ye further! When Cairtre's daughter
Saw what a fate had o'erta'en her Brave,
Her eyes became as twin founts of water,
Her heart again as a darker grave.

Clasp now thy lover, unhappy maiden!
But, see! thy sire tears thine arms away,
And in a dungeon, all anguish laden,
Shalt thou be cast ere the shut of day.

But what shall be in the sad years coming
Thy doom? I know not, but guess too well
That sunlight never shall trace thee roaming
Ayond the gloom of thy sunken cell!

This is the tale of the Prince of Oriel
And Darvorgilla, both sprung of Kings!
I trace it here as a dark memorial
Of how much woe thoughtless folly brings.

[1] *H.saoil se mar teoirneach;* he thought like thunder; i.e., the thought came on him like a thunderbolt.

[2] Alas!

[3] Pronounced *Mo vrone,* and means "My grief!"

[4] Royal neck-ornaments.

[5] Calbhach-proper name of a man; derived from Calb - bald-pated.

[6] Dundalk.

[7] Martha.

# A HIGHWAY FOR FREEDOM

AIR - *"Boyne Water."*

## I.

"My suffering country shall be freed,
    And shine with tenfold glory!"
So spake the gallant Winkelried,
    Renowned in German story.
"No tyrant, even of kingly grade,
    Shall cross or darken my way!"
Out flashed his blade, and so he made
For Freedom's course a highway!

## II.

We want a man like this, with pow'r
    To rouse the world by one word;
We want a chief to meet the hour,
    And march the masses onward.
But, chief or none, through blood and fire,
    My fatherland, lies thy way!
The men must fight who dare desire
    For Freedom's course a highway !

## III.

Alas! I can but idly gaze
    Around in grief and wonder,
The people's will alone can raise
    The people's shout of thunder.
Too long, my friends, you faint for fear,
    In secret crypt and by-way;
At last be men! Stand forth and clear
For Freedom's course a highway!

## IV.

You intersect wood, lea, and lawn,
    With roads for monster waggons,
Wherein you speed like lightning drawn
    By fiery iron dragons
So do. Such work is good, no doubt;
    But why not seek some nigh way
For mind as well? Path also out
    For Freedom's course a highway

## V.

Yes! up! and let your weapons be
    Sharp steel and self-reliance!
Why waste your burning energy
In void and vain defiance,
And phrases fierce but fugitive?
    'Tis deeds, not words, that I weigh -
Your swords and guns alone can give
To Freedom's course a highway!

# NOONDAY DREAMING

There danceth adown the mountain
The child of a lofty race,
A streamlet fresh from its fountain
Hies towards the valley apace.

Some fairy had whispered 'follow!'
And I have obeyed her well;
I tread the blossomy hollow
With my pilgrim staff and shell.

On, on, behold me straying,
And ever beside the stream,
As I list to its murmurous playing
And mark how its wavelets gleam.

Can this be the path I intended?
O, Sorceress! what shall I say?
Thy dazzle and music blended
Have wiled my reason away!

No mortal sounds are winging
Their wonted way along;
O, no! some Naiad is singing
A flattering summer-song.

# LINES WRITTEN IN A NUNNERY CHAPEL

Me hither from noonlight
    A voice ever calls
Where pale pillars cluster
And organ tones roll-
Nor sunlight nor moonlight
    E'er silvers these walls
Lives here other lustre-
    The Light of the Soul.

Here budded and blossomed
    Here faded and died
Like brief blooming roses
    Earth's purest of pure!
Now ever embosomed
    In bliss they abide
Oh! may, when Life closes,
    My meed be as sure!

# WISDOM AND FOLLY

They who go forth, and finally win
Their way to the Temple of Truth by Error's multiplied stages,
   They are the Sages!

They who stop short for life at some inn
On the side of the road-say Momus's, Mammon's, or Cupid's,
   They are the Stupids !

# KATHLEEN NI HOULAHAN

*(Another Version)*

In vain, in vain, we turn to Spain; she heeds us not;
Yet may we still, by strength of will, amend our lot;
O yes! our foe shall yet lie low; our swords are drawn
    For her, our queen, our Caitilin Ny Uallachain!

Yield not to fear, the time is near. With sword in hand
We soon shall chase the Saxon race far from our land.
What glory then to stand as men on field and bawn
    And see, all sheen, our Caitilin Ny Uallachain!

How tossed, how lost, with hopes all crossed, we long have been;
    Our gold is gone; gear have we none, as all have seen.
But ships shall brave the ocean wave, and morn shall dawn
    On Eire green, on Caitilin Ny Uallachain!

Let none believe that lovely Eve outworn or old;
Fair is her form, her blood is warm, her heart is bold!
Tho' strangers long have wrought her wrong, she will not fawn,
    Will not prove mean, our Caitilin Ny Uallachain!

Her stately air, her flowing hair, her eyes that far
Pierce thro' the gloom of Banba's doom, each like a star;
Her songful voice that makes rejoice hearts grief hath gnawn,
    Prove her our queen, our Caitilin Ny Uallachain!

We will not bear the chains we wear, not bear them long!
We seem bereaven, but mighty Heaven will make us strong:
    The God who led thro' Ocean Red all Israel on!
    Will aid our queen, our Caitilin Ny Uallachain!

**PART TWO**

# A selection of Famous Irish Poems and Songs

## By

# Noted Poets and Songwriters.

# THE "WILD GEESE"

*(A Lament for the Irish Jacobites)*

I have heard the curlew crying
By a lonely moor and mere
And the seagull's shriek in the gloaming
Is a lonely sound in the ear;
And I've heard the brown thrush mourning
For her children stol'n away
But its Oh, for the homeless "Wild Geese"
That sailed ere the dawn of the day

For the curlew, out on the moorland,
Hath five fine eggs in her nest;
And the thrush will get her a new love,
And sing her song with the best;
As the swallow flies to the summer
Will the gull return to the sea;
But never the wings of the "Wild Geese"
Will flash over hill and lea.

And it's ill to be roaming, roaming
With the homesick in the breast;
And it's long I'll look for your coming,
And my heart is your empty nest;
Oh' sore in the land of the stranger
They'll pine for the land far away;
And the day of Aughrim, my sorrow!
It was thou wert the bitter day!

*Katharine Tynan Hinkson (1861-1931)*

*Katharine Tynan Kinkson was one of the most noted poetesses and prose writers of her time. She was born in Clondalkin, County Dublin in 1861. Her poetry is marked by sincere love of her country and religious feeling. She has published over eighty volumes of prose and verse. Her poem Lament for the Irish Jacobites "The Wild Geese" must be included in any collection of Irish poems.*

***The Day of Aughrim*** *Aughrim is a small village in County Galway. Here the Williamite General Ginkel defeated St Ruth who was in command of the Irish forces of King James on July 12th 1691, after the battles of the Boyne, Aughrim and the treaty of Limerick Patrick Sarsfield and more than 20,000 Irish who had fought gallantly for King James left Ireland for ever and joined the armies of France, they formed the nucleus of the famous 'Irish Brigade'.*

# THE LAMENT OF THE IRISH EMIGRANT

I'm sitting on the stile, Mary, where we sat side by side,
On a bright May morning, long ago, when first you were my bride.
The corn was springing fresh and green, and the lark sang loud and high,
And the red was on your lip, Mary, and the love light in your eye.

The place is little changed, Mary, the day as bright as then,
The lark's loud song is in my ear and the corn is green again!
But I miss the soft clasp of your hand, and your breath warm on my cheek;
And I still keep listening for the words you never more may speak!

Tis but a step down yonder lane, and the little church stands near,
The church where we were wed, Mary - I see the spire from here;
But the graveyard lies between, Mary, and my step might break your rest;
For I've laid you, darling, down to sleep, with your baby on your breast.

I'm lonely now, Mary, for the poor make no new friends;
But, oh! they love the better far the few our Father sends!
And you were all I had, Mary, my blessing and my pride;
There's nothing left to care for now, since my poor Mary died.

Yours was the brave good heart, Mary, that still kept hoping on,
When trust in God had left my soul, and my arm's young strength had gone:
There was comfort ever on your lip, and the kind look on your brow;
I bless you for the same, Mary, though you cannot hear me now.

I thank you for that patient smile, when your heart was like to break,
When the hunger-pain was gnawing there, and you hid it for my sake
I bless you for the pleasant word, when your heart was sad and sore,
O! I'm thankful you are gone, Mary, where grief can't reach you more!

I'm bidding you a long farewell, my Mary - kind and true!
But I'll not forget you, darling, in the land I'm going to;
They say there's bread and work for all, and the sun shines ever there,
But I'll not forget old Ireland, were it fifty times as fair!

And often in those grand old woods I'll sit and shut my eyes,
And my heart will travel back again to the place where Mary lies;
And I'll think I see the little stile where we sat side by side,
And the springing corn, and the bright May morn when first you were my bride.

*Lady Dufferin*

*Lady Dufferin (1807-1863). Grand-daughter of Richard Sheridan and sister of the Duchess of Somerset. Well known in fashionable society for her wit and beauty. The best known of her many popular ballads and songs is the 'Lament of the Irish Emigrant' which will keep her memory ever dear to the Irish people.*

# CUISLE MO CHROIDHE[1]

Dear Erin, how sweetly thy green bosom rises!
An emerald set in the ring of the sea
Each blade of thy meadows my faithful heart prizes,
Thou queen of the west! the world's Cuisle mo chroidhe.

Thy gates open wide to the poor and the stranger
There smiles hospitality, hearty and free;
Thy friendship is seen in the moment of danger
And the wand'rer is welcomed with Cuisle mo chroidhe.

Thy sons they are brave; but, the battle once over,
In brotherly peace with their foes they agree;
And the roseate cheeks of thy daughters discover
The soul-speaking blush that says Cuisle mo chroidhe.

Then flourish forever, my dear native Erin!
While sadly I wander an exile from thee,
And, firm in thy mountains, no injury fearing,
May heaven defend its own Cuisle mo chroidhe.

*John Philpot Curran (1750-1817)*

[1] 'Vein of My Heart'

*Brilliant Irish advocate and political orator. Born at Newmarket Co Cork.A noted member of the "Patriotic Party" in the Irish parliament. Unsuccessfully defended Wolfe Tone In 1798, Tone committed suicide in his cell, and cheated the hangman. Curran died in London. In 1843 his remains were transferred to Ireland and buried in Glasnevin Cemetery Dublin.*

# THE OLD LAND

Ah kindly and sweet we must love thee, perforce!
The disloyal, the coward alone would not love thee;
Oh, mother of heroes! strong mother! soft nurse!
We are thine while the the large clouds swim onward above thee!
By thy ever blue that draw heaven so near;
By thy cliffs, by thy lakes, by thine ocean-lulled highlands!
And more by thy records disastrous and dear,
The shrines on thy headlands, the cells in thine islands!

Ah well sings the thrush by Lixnau and Triagh-li!
Ah well breaks the wave upon Umbhall and Brandon!
Thy breeze o'er the uplands blows clement and free,
And o'er fields once his own which the hind must now abandon,
A caitiff the noble who draws from thy plains
His all, yet reveres not the source of his greatness;
A clown and a serf, mid his boundless domains,
His spirit consumes in the prison of his straightness!

Through the cloud of its pathos thy face is more fair:
In old time thou wert sun-clad: the gold robe thou worest;
To thee the heart turns as the deer to its lair
Ere she dies, her first bed in the gloom of the forest.
Our glory, our sorrow, our mother! Thy God
In thy worst dereliction forsook but to prove thee:
Blind, blind as the blindworm; cold, cold as the clod,
Who seeing thee, see not, possess, but not love thee!

*Aubrey De Vere (1814-1902)*

*Another moving poem about Heroes, cowards, sorrow, and olden times in Ireland.*
*'Lixnau, Traigli' = Lixnaw and Tralee in Co Kerry, 'Umbhall' = West of Mayo.*
*Caitiff = coward, craven.*

# SHE IS FAR FROM THE LAND

She is far from the land where her young hero sleeps,
And lovers around her are sighing;
But coldly she turns from their gaze and weeps,
For her heart in his grave is lying.

She sings the wild songs of her dear native plains,
Every note which he lov'd awaking;
Ah! little they think, who delight in her strains,
How the heart of the minstrel is breaking.

He had lived for his love, for his country he died,
They were all that to life had entwined him;
Nor soon shall the tears of his country be dried,
Nor long will his love stay behind him.

Oh! make her a grave where the sunbeams rest
When they promise a glorious morrow;
They'll shine o'er her sleep, like a smile from the West,
From her own loved island of sorrow.

*Thomas Moore (1780-1852)*

*This is a sad poem about Sarah Curran, who was betrothed to Robert Emmet, after his execution in Dublin following a rebellion in 1803, she left Ireland forever and died of a broken heart. This is a very sad and lovely story of true love, heartbreak and sorrow.*

# A BALLAD OF ATHLONE

Does any man dream that a Gael can fear?
Of a thousand deeds let him learn but one!
The Shannon swept onward broad and clear,
Between the leaguers and broad Athlone.

'Break down the bridge!' Six warriors rushed
Through storm of shot and storm of shell:
With late but certain victory flushed
The grim Dutch gunners eyed them well.

They wrench'd at the planks mid a hail of fire :
They fell in death their work half done :
The bridge stood fast; and nigh and nigher
The foe swarmed darkly, densely on.

Oh, who for Erin will strike a stroke?
Who hurl yon planks where the waters roar?
Six warriors forth from their comrades broke,
And flung themselves on that bridge once more.

Again at the rocking planks they dashed;
And four dropped dead; and two remained :
The huge beams groaned, the arch down-crashed;
Two stalwart swimmers the margin gained.

St. Ruth in his stirrups stood up, and cried,
'I have seen no deed like that in France!'
With a toss of his head, Sarsfield replied,
' They had luck the dogs!' 'Twas a merry chance!'

O many a year on Shannon's side,
They sang upon moor and they sang upon heath,
Of the twain that breasted the raging tide,
And the ten that shook bloody hands with death!

*Aubrey De Vere*

*Aubrey De Vere (1814-1902). Third son of Sir Aubrey De Vere of Curragh Chase Co Limerick. Author of many works in prose and verse. His most interesting poetical work for Irish readers is 'Innisfail' a series of poems conveying a picture of certain great epochs in Irish history. During the siege of Athlone 1691 the Williamite General Ginkel led the army of William of Orange, Athlone was held by General St Ruth and Patrick Sarsfield for King James 11. This is a stirring story Of outstanding bravery and heroism by Sarsfield's Irish soldiers.*

# NATIONALITY

A nation's voice, a nation's voice
It is a solemn thing!
It bonds the bondage sick rejoice
Tis stronger than a king.
Tis like the light of many stars;
The sound of many waves;
Which brightly looks through prison bars,
And sweetly sounds in caves.
Yet it is noblest, godliest known,
When righteous triumph swells its tone.


A nations flag, a nations flag
If wickedly unrolled,
May foes in adverse battle drag
Its every fold from fold.
But in the cause of Liberty,
Guard it 'gainst Earth and Hell
Guard it till Death or Victory
Look you guard it well!
No saint or king has tomb so proud,
As he whose flag becomes his shroud.


A nation's right, a nation's right
God gave it, and gave, too,
A nation's sword, a nation's might,
Danger to guard it through.
Tis freedom from a foreign yoke,
Tis just and equal laws,
Which deal unto the humblest folk,
As in a noble cause.
On nations fixed in right and truth,
God would bestow eternal youth.

May Irelands voice be ever heard
Amid the world's applause!
And never be her flag-staff stirred,
But in an honest cause!
May freedom be her very breath,
Be justice ever dear
And never an ennobled death
May son of Erin fear!
So the Lord God will ever smile,
With guardian grace upon our Isle.

*Thomas Davis (1814-1845)*

*Thomas Davis was an ideal Irishman, ardent generous and unselfish, he died at the early age of thirty and was mourned by his countrymen of every creed and political party, Nationality stresses deep love of ones Country and its history.*

# MICHAEL DWYER

And now Michael Dwyer you and your gallant men
Are hunted through the valley and tracked into the glen
Sleep not but watch and listen keep ready blade and ball
The soldiers know you hide tonight in the glen of wild Imall


The soldiers searched the valley and towards the dawn of day
Discovered where the outlaws the dauntless rebels lay
Around the little cottage they formed into a ring
And called out 'Michael Dwyer surrender to the King';


Then answered Michael Dwyer-'into this house we came
Unasked by those who own it; they cannot be to blame.
Then let these guiltless people, unquestioned, pass you through
And when they've passed in safety, I'll tell you what we'll do.'


T'was done. 'and now' said Dwyer, 'Your dirty work begin;
You are a hundred outside – we're only four within ;
We've heard your haughty summons, and this is our reply –
We're true United Irishmen! We'll fight until we die!


Then burst the war's red lightning! Then poured the leaden rain!
The hills around re-echoed the thunder-peals again;
The soldiers falling round him, brave Dwyer sees with pride,
But, ah! One gallant comrade is wounded by his side.


Yet there are three remaining, good battle still to do;
Their hands are strong and steady, their aim is quick and true.
But hark that furious shouting the savage soldiers raise!
The house is fired around them! The roof is all ablaze!

And brighter every moment the lurid flame arose,
And loudly swelled the laughter and cheering of their foes;
Then spake the brave Mc Allister, the weak and wounded man,
'You can escape my comrades, and this shall be your plan;

'Place in my hands a musket, then lie upon the floor.
I'll stand before the soldiers and open wide the door;
They'll pour into my heart boys, the fire of their array;
Then while their guns are empty, dash through them, and away!

He stood before the Yoemen revealed amidst the flame;
From out their levelled muskets the wished for volley came.
Up sprang the three survivors for whom the hero died,
But only Michael Dwyer burst the ranks outside.

He baffled his pursuers, who followed like the wind.
He swam the river Slaney, and left them far behind.
But many a scarlet soldier he promised soon would fall
For those, his gallant comrades, who died in wild Imaal.

*Timothy D Sullivan (1827-1914)*

*He was born in Bantry, Co. Cork. Politician, poet, and journalist. Contributed to the 'Nation' and eventually owned and edited the journal. He was a very popular poet, and became a Member of Parliament for County Donegal, and County Westmeath for many years. He was also Lord Mayor of Dublin in 1886 and 1887.*

*Michael Dwyer was a United Irishman, who after the rebellion of 1798 carried on with the fight in his native Wicklow Mountains, this ballad tells of his escape after being hunted with his men and surrounded in a cottage in the Glen of Imaal, near Donard in County Wicklow. After a fierce battle, one of his companions Sam McAllister, was badly wounded he opened the door and sacrificed himself to save the others, Michael Dwyer was the only one to break clear, the others were captured and eventually hanged. It is believed that he escaped to Australia, where he spent the rest of his life. The cottage was preserved and is now open to the public. In Baltinglass County Wicklow a statue now stands, in memory of the heroic bravery, and sacrifice of Sam McAllister.*

# FLAG OF SINN FEIN

They raised a great standard of hope for the nation,
Their strong arms bracing its staff to the breeze,
And proudly they bore it mid scenes of elation
Defending it bravely where foes would it seize.
Soon over each town and each village 'twas waving,
In far-scattered hamlets on hillside and plain,
And the young men of Ireland arose from their slaving
To march and to fight 'neath the flag of Sinn Fein.

When Pearse led his comrades that day by the Liffey
Behind it they marched with a soldierly mien,
And soon over Dublin's great fortress 'twas flying -
The hope of the nation, White, Orange and Green.
Beneath it fought men who were proud to be shedding
Their blood, ever mindful 'twould not flow in vain,
Each man a bridegroom at Dark Rosaleen's wedding
As bravely they died 'neath the flag of Sinn Fein.

In the fresh breeze of morning it floated in glory,
In the lull of the night by its staff it reclined,
In the hour of surrender - no hand free to save it
Lead-sprayed and shell-torn to the flames 'twas consigned.
Through the night the fire laboured, dawn saw the roof caving,
Then the smoke cleared away and the sun shone again,
And above the gaunt ruin, still defiantly waving
Was that battle-scarred emblem, the flag of Sinn Fein.

*Conleith Martin*

*A really wonderful and touching lyric, beautifully written about the Easter Rising of 1916. The brave patriotic young men who though they knew they could not win were prepared to die for Ireland, and in many cases, sadly they did. But they laid the foundation stone for the future, and as Patrick Pearse said at his court martial, we seem to have lost, we have not lost, to refuse to fight would have been to lose. If our deed has not been sufficient to win freedom for our country, then our children will win it with a better deed. And Pearse's words proved prophetic. In 1919 the young men of Ireland raised the flag of liberty and freed their native land.*

# BOOLAVOGUE

At Boolavogue as the sun was setting
O'er the bright May meadows of Shelmalier,
A rebel hand set the heather blazing
And brought the neighbours from far and near.
Then Father Murphy, from old Kilcormack,
Spurred up the rocks with 'a warning cry:
"Arm! Arm!" he cried "for I've come to lead you
For Ireland's freedom we live and die."

He led us on 'gainst the coming soldiers,
And cowardly Yeomen we put to flight
'Twas at the Harrow the boys of Wexford
Showed Bookeys regiment how men could fight.
Look out for hirelings, King George of England,
Search every kingdom where breathes a slave.
For Father Murphy from the County Wexford
Sweeps o'er the land like a mighty wave.

We took Camolin and Enniscorthy,
And Wexford storming drove out our foes;
'Twas at Sliabh Coillte our pikes were reeking
With the crimson stream of the beaten Yeos.
At Tubberneering and Ballyellis
Full many a Hessian lay in his gore
Ah, Father Murphy, had aid come over,
The green flag floated from shore to shore!

At Vinegar Hill, o'er the pleasant Slaney,
Our heroes vainly stood back to back.
And the Yeos. at Tullow took Father Murphy
And burned his body upon the rack.
God grant you glory, brave Father Murphy,
And open heaven to all your men;
The cause that called you may call to-morrow
In another fight for the green again.

*P J McCall (1861-1919)*

*Boolavogue is the story of the rising of 1798 in Wexford led by Fr. John Murphy. It was a gallant effort against overwhelming odds, and will always be remembered with pride, in fact they very nearly won. Their names will always be honoured by the people of Ireland. The poem is in itself a wonderful history lesson and tribute to their heroic deeds, and sacrifice for love of their Country.*

# ASPIRATIONS OF YOUTH

Higher, higher will we climb
Up the mount of glory,
That our names may live through time
In our country's story;
Happy, when her welfare calls,
He who conquers, he who falls.

Deeper, deeper let us toil
In the mines of knowledge;
Nature's wealth and Learning's spoil
Win from school and college;
Delve we there for richer gems
Than the stars of diadems.

Onward, onward may we press
Through the path of duty;
Virtue is true happiness,
Excellence true beauty;
Minds are of celestial birth,
Make we then a heaven of earth.

Closer, closer let us knit
Heart and hands together,
Where our fireside-comforts sit
In the wildest weather;
O, they wander wide who roam
For the joys of life from home.

*James Montgomery (1771-1854)*

*Wrote a large amount of verse and hymns, his chief claim to distinction are the beautiful hymns he wrote, which were published in about 1850.*

# THE BELLS OF SHANDON

With deep affection and recollection
I often think of the Shandon bells,
With sounds so wild would, in days of childhood,
Fling round my cradle their magic spells-
On this I ponder, where'er I wander,
And thus grow fonder, sweet Cork of thee ;
With thy bells of Shandon,
That sound so grand on
The pleasant waters of river Lee.


I have heard bells chiming, full many a clime in,
Tolling sublime in cathedral shrine ;
While at a glib rate brass tongues would vibrate,
But all their music spoke naught to thine
For memory dwelling on each proud swelling
Of thy belfry knelling its bold notes free,
Made the bells of Shandon,
Sound far more grand on
The pleasant waters of the river Lee.


I have heard the bells tolling 'old Adrian's mole' in
Their thunder rolling from the Vatican
With cymbals glorious, swinging uproarious
In the gorgeous turrets of Notre Dame ;
But thy sounds were sweeter than the dome of Peter
Flings o'er the Tiber, pealing solemnly.
O! the bells of Shandon,
Sound far more grand on
The pleasant waters of the river Lee.

There's a bell in Moscow, while on tower and kiosko,
In St. Sophia the Turkman gets,
And loud in air calls men to prayer,
From the tapering summits of tall minarets.
Such empty phantom I freely grant them,
But there's an anthem more dear to me,
It's the bells of Shandon,
That sound so grand on
The pleasant waters of the river Lee.

*Rev. Francis Mahony ('Father Prout') (1804-1866)*

*Fr. Mahony. Better known by his 'non de plume' of 'Father Prout' eminent scholar and wit. Born in Cork. Admitted to Orders in 1832 , he soon abandoned his clerical duties, and concentrated solely on literature and journalism.*
*Old Adrian' mole = the tomb of Adrian, part of the castle of St. Angelo at Rome.*
*Notre Dame = Cathedral in Paris. Kiosko = an Eastern garden pavilion.*
*Minarets = turrets on a Mahommedan place of worship.*

# THE MINSTREL BOY

The Minstrel boy to the war has gone
In the ranks of death you will find him
His fathers sword he has girded on
And his wild harp is slung behind him
Land of song said the warrior bard
Though all the world betrayed you
One sword at least thy right shall guard
And one faithful harp will praise you.

The Minstrel fell but the foemans chains
Could not put his proud soul under
The harp he loved ne'er spoke again
For he tore its chords asunder
And said no chain shall sully thee
Thou soul of love and bravery
Thy songs were made for pure and free
They shall never sound in slavery

*Thomas Moore (1780-1852)*

*Moore was born in Dublin, educated at Trinity College. In 1799 he moved to London. His 'Irish Melodies' are his most popular and 'The Minstrel Boy ' is loved , sung, and recited around the world by people of Irish descent.*

# THE JACKETS GREEN

When I was a maiden young and fair on the pleasant banks of Lee,
No bird that in the greenwood sang was half so blithe and free,
No heart ne'er leaped to flying feet, no love sang me his Queen.
Till down the glen rode Sarsfields men, and they wore their jackets green.

Young Donal sat on his gallant grey like a king on a royal seat,
And my heart leapt out on its regal way to worship at his feet ;
O love had you come in those colours dressed and wooed with a soldiers mein,
I'd have laid my head on your throbbing breast for the sake of your jacket green.

No hoarded wealth did my true love own save the good sword that he bore ;
But I loved him for himself alone and the colours that he wore.
For had he come in England's red to make me England's Queen,
I'd have roved the high green hills instead for the sake of his jacket green.

When William stormed with shot and shell at the walls of Garryowen,
In the breach my Donal fell and he sleeps near the Treaty Stone.
That breach the foemen never crossed while he swung his broadsword keen,
But I do not weep my darling lost for he fell 'neath the Flag of Green.

When Sarsfield sailed away I wept as I heard the wild ochone,
I felt then dead as the men who slept 'neath the walls of Garryowen.
While Ireland held my Donal blest no wild seas rolled between,
I could fold him to my breast all robed in his jacket green.

O Ireland, sad on thy lonely soul there breaks the winter sea,
But sadder and higher the wild waves roll from the hearts that break for thee.
Yet grief shall come from thy heartless foes, and their thrones in the dust be seen,
So Irish maids love none but those who wear the jacket green.

*Michael Scanlan (1836-1908)*

*Michael Scanlan was born in Limerick , he wrote many poems including 'The bold Fenian men' 'Limerick is beautiful' and 'A day in Eirinn'. 'The Jackets Green' is a wonderful example of his talent. A story of the siege of Limerick at the time of the battles of the Boyne and Aughrim during the war of King William of Orange and King James, the Treaty Stone still stands in Limerick, as a memorial to Patrick Sarsfield 'Lord Lucan' who after the signing of the Treaty left Ireland forever with about 20,000 of his men.*

# LET ERIN REMEMBER

Let Erin remember the days of old
'Ere her faithless sons betrayed her;
When Malachy wore the collar of gold
Which he won from the proud invader;
When her kings with standards of green unfurled,
Led the Red Branch Knights to danger.
'Ere the Emerald Gem of the Western World
Was set in the crown of a stranger.


On Lough Neagh's Banks as the fisherman strays,
In the clear cold eve declining
He sees the round towers of other days
In the waves beneath him shining ;
Thus shall memory often in dreams sublime
Catch a glimpse of days that are over,
Thus sighing , look through the waves of time
For the long faded glories they cover.

*Thomas Moore (1780-1852)*

*Another meaningful poem from Thomas Moore, it tells of a fisherman looking into the waters of Lough Neaghs banks and seeing glimpses of the past, he sees the Majesty of Ireland long ago, and tells us it is not to be forgotten. He tells of Malachy, the Red Branch Knights and the glory of Ireland in days of yore.*

# O'DONNELL ABU

Proudly the notes of the trumpet are sounding,
Loudly the war-cries arise on the gale;
Fleetly the steed by Lough Swuiligh is bounding,
To join the thick squadrons in Saimear's green vale.
On, every mountaineer,
Strangers to flight and fear,
Rush to the standard of dauntless Red Hugh!
Bonnought and gallowglass
Throng from each mountain pass,
On for old Erin -O'Donnell abu!


Princely O'Neill to our aid is advancing,
With many a chieftain and warrior clan;
A thousand proud steeds in his vanguard are prancing
'Neath the borderers brave from the banks of the Bann.
Many a heart shall quail
Under its coat of mail,
Deeply the merciless foeman shall rue,
When on his ear shall ring,
Borne on the breeze's wing
Tir-Chonaill's dread war-cry - O'Donnell abu!


Wildly o'er Desmond the war-wolf is howling,
Fearless the eagle sweeps over the plane;
The fox in the streets of the city is prowling,
And all who would scare them are banished or slain.
Grasp every stalwart hand,
Hackbut and battle-brand,
Pay them all back the deep debt so long due;
Norris and Clifford well
Can of Tir-Chonaill tell
Onward to glory - O'Donnell abu!

Sacred the cause that Clann-Chonaill's defending
The altars we kneel at, the homes of our sires;
Ruthless the ruin the foe is extending,
Midnight is red with the plunderer's fires.
On with O'Donnell then,
Fight the old fight again.
Sons of Tir-Chonaill, all valiant and true;
Make the false Saxon feel
Erin's avenging steel,
Strike for your country -O'Donnell abu!

*M J McCann*

*An Irish battle song written about 1843.Hugh O'Donnell, Earl of Tyr-Connell, a large part of north west Ulster. O'Donnell and Hugh O'Neill his neighbour and Earl of Tyrone put up the last Irish resistance to the English Queen Elizabeth, and her plan for the Plantations of Ulster and seizure of their lands, to be distributed amongst Scottish and English settlers. O'Neill and O'Donnell left Ireland forever in what became known as the flight of the Earls, in 1607.*

*Bonnought = Irish Mercenary. Gallowglass = Scottish Mercenary of Norse descent, they usually fought in armour and with battleaxes, they were ferocious fighters and much feared by their enemies.*

# THE BATTLE EVE OF THE BRIGADE

The mess-tent is full and the glasses are set,
And the gallant Count Thomond is president yet,
The vet'ran arose, like an uplifted lance,
Crying: 'Comrades, a health to the monarch of France!'
With bumpers and cheers they have done as they bade,
For King Louis is loved by the Irish Brigade.

'A health to King James', and they bent as they quaffed,
'Here's to George the Elector', and fiercely they laughed,
'Good luck to the girls we wooed long ago,
Where Shannon, and Barrow and Avondhu flow;
'God prosper Old Ireland' you'd think them afraid,
So pale grew the cheeks of the Irish Brigade.

But surely, that light cannot come from our lamp?
And that noise are they all getting drunk in the camp?
'Hurrah' boys the morning of battle is come;
And the general's beating on many a drum.
So they rush from the revel to join the parade,
For the van is the right of the Irish Brigade.

So they fought as they revelled fast, fiery, and true,
And though victors, left on the field not a few:
And they, who survived, fought and drank as of yore,
But the land of their heart's hope they never saw more.
For in far foreign fields from Dunkirk to Belgrade.
Lie the soldiers and chiefs of the Irish Brigade.

*Thomas Davis (1814-1845)*

*The Irish Brigade was formed by soldiers in the army of King James 11. They left Ireland with Patrick Sarsfield (Lord Lucan) after the capitulation at Limerick, and fought with the army of King Louis XIV of France. George the Elector, was King George of England, who was Elector of Hanover. James, was James 11 defeated at the Boyne and Aughrim, who afterwards went into exile.*

# GOUGAUNE BARRA

There is a green island in lone Gougaune Barra
Where Allua of songs rushes forth as an arrow;
In deep-valleyed Desmond A thousand wild fountains
Come down to that lake from their home in the mountains.
There grows the wild ash, and the time stricken willow
Looks chidingly down on the mirth of the billow;
As, like some gay child, the sad monitor scorning,
It lightly laughs back to the laugh of the morning.


And its zone of dark hills O' to see them all bright'ning,
When the tempest flings out its red banner of lightning,
And the waters rush down, mid the thunder's deep rattle,
Like clans from their hills at the voice of the battle;
And brightly the fire-crested billows are gleaming,
And wildly from Mullagh the eagles are screaming.
O, where is the dwelling in valley or highland,
So meet for a bard as this lone little island?


How oft when the summer sun rested on Clara,
And lit the dark heath on the hills of Ivera,
Have I sought thee, sweet spot, from my home by the ocean,
And trod all thy wilds with a minstrel's devotion,
And though of thy bards, when assembling together
In the cleft of thy rocks, or the depth of thy heather;
They fled from the Saxon's dark bondage and slaughter,
And waked their last song by the rush of thy water.


High sons of the lyre, O' how proud was the feeling,
To think while alone through that solitary stealing,
Though loftier Minstrels green Erin can number,
I only awoke your wild harp from its slumber,
And mingled once more with the voice of those fountains
The songs even echo forgot on her mountains;
And gleaned every grey legend, that darkly was sleeping
Where the mist and the rain o'er their beauty were creeping.

Least bard of the hills! were it mine to inherit
The fire of thy harp, and the wing of thy spirit,
With the wrongs which like thee to our country have bound me,
Did your mantle of song fling its radiance around me,
Still, still in those wilds might young liberty rally,
And send her strong shout over mountain and valley,
The star of the west might yet rise in its glory,
And the land that was darkest be brighter in story.


I too shall be gone; but my name shall be spoken
When Erin awakes and her fetters are broken;
Some Minstrel will come, in the summers eve's gleaming,
When freedoms young light on his spirit is beaming,
And bend o'er my grave with a tear of emotion,
Where calm Avon-Buee seeks the kisses of ocean,
Or plant a wild wreath, from the banks of that river,
O,er the heart and the harp that are sleeping forever.


*J J Callanan (1795-1829)*

*A lovely poem about 'Gougaune Barra. Callanan was born in Cork. He spent many years amid the romantic Mountains of West Cork collecting a store of legendary lore he died in Lisbon. This poem is one of the most popular Irish poems, and is well remembered by many an Irish exile in many parts of the World. Gougaune Barra is situated in the mountains on the Kealkil-Pass of Keimeineigh-Ballingeary road, the meaning of the name is, the hollow or recess of Saint Finbarr.*

# MY GRAVE

Shall they bury me deep
Where wind-forgetting waters sleep?
Shall they dig a grave for me
Under the green-wood tree?
Or on the wild heath
Of the storm doth blow?
Oh, no! Oh, no!

Shall they bury me in the Palace Tombs,
Or under the shade of Cathedral domes?
Sweet 'twere to lie on Italy's shore;
Yet not there nor in Greece, though I love it more
In the wolf or the vulture my grave shall I find?
Shall my ashes career on the world seeing wind?
Shall they fling my corpse in the battle mound
Where coffinless thousands lie under the ground?
Just as they fall they are buried so
Oh, no! Oh, no!

No! on an Irish green-hill-side,
On an opening lawn – but not too wide ;
For I love the drip of the wetted trees
I love not the gales, but a gentle breeze
To freshen the turf – put no tombstone there,
But green sods decked with daisies fair ;
Nor sods too deep, but so that the dew
The matted grass roots may trickle through.
Be my epitaph writ on my country's mind,
'He served his country, and loved his kind'

Oh! twere merry unto the grave to go,
If one were sure to be buried so.

*Thomas Davis (1814 –1845)*

*Born at Mallow Co Cork, And educated at Trinity College Dublin. He was called to the bar in 1838. He took part in the founding of the 'Nation' with Charles Gavin Duffy , and John Blake Dillon, and contributed to its columns in prose and verse. He was a brilliant member of the Young Ireland Party. He was a sad loss to his friends and country when he died at the early age of thirty.*

# SALUTATION TO THE KELTS

Hail to our Keltic brethren! wherever they may be,
In the far woods of Oregon or o'er the Atlantic sea;
Whether they guard the banner of St George in the Indian Vales,
Or spread beneath the nightless North experimental sails-
One in name and in fame
Are the sea divided Gaels,

Though fallen the state of Erin, and changed the Scottish land,
Though small the power of Mona, though unwaked Llewellyn's band,
Though Ambrose Merlin's prophecies are held as idle tales,
Though Iona's ruined cloisters are swept by northern gales:
One in name and in fame
Are the sea divided Gaels.

In Northern Spain and Italy our brethern also dwell,
And brave are the traditions of their fathers that they tell :
The Eagle or the Crescent in the dawn of history pales
Before the advancing banners of the great Roman conquering Gaels.
One in name and in fame
Are the sea divided Gaels.

A greeting and a promise unto them all we send;
Their character our charter is, their glory is our end.
Their friend shall be our friend, our foe whoe'er assails
The glory or the story of the sea divided Gaels.
One in name and in fame
Are the sea divided Gaels.

*Thomas D'Arcy Mc Gee (1825-1868)*

*A poem and tribute to the ancient Kelts and Gaels, ancestors of the Irish people, mighty Warriors in days of yore.*

*'Oregon' = one of the Pacific States of the USA.*
*'Mona' = Anglesey an island off the coast of Wales in the Irish Sea.*
*'Llewellyn' = The last prince of North Wales reigned from 1246 to 1282.*
*'Ambrose Merlin regarded as magician and prophet about the year 480.' Iona one of the Western Scottish islands where the ancient monastry of St Columba was founded about 565'.*
*'The Eagle and the Crescent', the eagle was the ensign of the ancient Kings of Babylon and Persia, the Crescent represented Turkish power.*

# KELLY OF KILLANNE

What's the news'? What's the news? O my bold Shelmalier,
With your long-barrelled gun of the sea?
Say what wind from the north blows his messenger here
With a hymn of the dawn for the free?
"Goodly news, goodly news, do I bring, youth of Forth;
Goodly news shall you hear, Bargy man!
For the boys march at morn from the South to the North,
Led by Kelly, the Boy from Killanne!"

"Tell me who is that giant with the gold curling hair
He who rides at the head of your band?
Seven feet is his height, with some inches to spare,
And he looks like a king in command!" -
"Ah, my lads, that's the pride of the bold Shelmaliers,
'Mong our greatest of heroes, a Man!
Fling your beavers aloft and give three ringing cheers
For John Kelly, the Boy from Killanne!"

Enniscorthy's in flames, and old Wexford is won,
And the Barrow to-morrow we cross,
On a hill o'er the town we have planted a gun
That will batter the gateways of Ross!
All the Forth men and Bargy men will march o'er the heath,
With brave Harvey to lead on the van;
But the foremost of all in the grim Gap of Death
Will be Kelly, the Boy from Killanne!

But the gold sun of Freedom grew darkened 'at Ross,
And it set by the Slaney's red waves;
And poor Wexford, stript naked, hung high on a cross,
And her heart pierced by traitors and slaves!
Glory O! Glory O! To her brave sons who died
For the cause of long-down-trodden man!
Glory O! to Mount Leinster's own darling and pride -
Dauntless Kelly, the Boy from Killanne!

*P J McCall (1861-1919)*

*John Kelly was an officer in the United Irishmen. He was the leader of the men from the West Wexford Barony of Bantry. He was a giant of a man well over six foot in height and a fighting ability to match He was badly wounded at New Ross, after the defeat at Vinegar Hill, he was taken from his bed in his sisters house at Wexford though severely wounded, tried by court-martial and hanged. He was a brave and fearless young Irishman who will live forever in song and story in the hearts of Irish people.*

# THE RECONCILIATION

The old man knelt at the altar,
His enemy's hand to take
And at first his weak voice did falter,
And his feeble limbs did shake;
For his only brave boy, his glory,
Had been stretched at the old mans feet,
A corpse-all so haggard and gory,
By the hand which he now must greet.

And soon the old man stopped speaking;
And the rage which had not gone by,
From under his brows came breaking
Up into his enemy's eye;
And now his limbs were not shaking;
His clench'd hand his bosom crossed;
He look'd a fierce wish, to be taking
Revenge for the boy he had lost!

But the old man looked around him,
And thought of the place he was in,
And thought of the promise that bound him,
And thought that revenge was sin;
And then crying tears like a woman,
'Your hand!' he said ay, that hand!
Oh I do forgive you, foeman,
For the sake of our bleeding land!

*John Banim (1798-1842)*

*Born in Kilkenny. Having showed a great talent for drawing and painting, he became a pupil at the Drawing Academy of the Royal Dublin Society. In 1815 he returned to Kilkenny, and after a long period of ill health devoted himself to literature, in Dublin and later in London, he distinguished himself as a dramatist poet and novelist. The Reconciliation a story of a fathers grief and lust for revenge, it then turns into forgiveness and realization of the sin and futility of revenge.*

# FAR- AWAY

As chimes that flow o'er shining seas
When Morn alights on meads of May,
Faint voices fill the western breeze
With whisp'ring songs from Far-Away.
Oh, dear the dells of Dunanore,
A home in odorous Ossory
But sweet as honey, running o'er,
The Golden Shore of Far-Away!

There grows the Tree whose summer breath
Perfumes with joy the azure air;
And he who feels it fears not death,
Nor longer heeds the hounds of Care.
Oh, soft the skies of Seskinore,
And mild is meadowy Mellaray;
But sweet as honey, running o'er,
The Golden Shore of Far-Away;

There sings the voice whose wondrous tune
Falls, like diamond-showers above,
That in the radiant dawn of June
Renew a world of Youth and Love.
Oh, fair the founts of Farranfore,
And bright is billowy Ballintrae;
But sweet as honey, running o'er,
The Golden Shore of Far-Away!

Come Fragrance of the Flowering Tree,
Oh, sing sweet Bird, thy magic lay,
Till all the world be young with me,
And love shall lead us far away.
Oh, dear the dells of Dunanore,
But sweet as honey, running o'er
The Golden Shore of Far-Away.

*George Sigerson*

*Descendant of a Norse-Irish family. He died in Dublin in 1925. He was President of the National Literary Society. Senator of the National University. He rendered everlasting service to the cause of native Irish Literature, and his translations from the Irish are unequalled.*

# A GAELIC SONG

A murmurous tangle of voices
Laughter to left and right,
We waited the curtain's rising
In a dazzling glare of light;
When down through through the din came, slowly,
Softly, then clear and strong,
The mournful minor cadence
Of a sweet old Gaelic song.


Like the trill of a lark new-risen,
It trembled upon the air,
And wondering eyes were lifted
To seek for the singer there;
Some dreamed of the thrush at noontide,
Some fancied a linnets wail,
While the notes went sobbing sighing,
O'er the heartstrings of the Gael.


The lights grew blurred and a vision
Fell upon all who heard,
The purple of moorland heather
By a wonderful wind was stirred;
Green rings of rushes went swaying,
Gaunt boughs of Winter made moan;
One saw the glory of Life go by,
And one saw Death alone.


A river twined through its shallows,
Cool waves crept up on a strand,
Or fierce, like a mighty army,
Swept wide on a conquered land;
The Dead left cairn and barrow,
And passed in noble train,
With sheltering shield, and slender spear,
Ere the curtain rose again.

The four great seas of Eire
Heaved under ships of war,
The God of battle befriended,
We saw the star! the star!
We nerved us for deeds of daring,
For Right we stood against Wrong;
We heard the prayers of our mothers,
In sweet old Gaelic song.


It was the soul of Eire
Awaking in speech she knew
When the clans held the glens and the mountains
And the hearts of their chiefs were true;
She hath stirred at last in her sleeping,
She is folding her dreams away,
The hour of her destiny neareth,
And it may be to-day – to-day.

*Ethna Carbery*

*'Ethna Carbery' is the nom de plume of Mrs. Anna Johnston Mac Manus. She died in 1902, and was a loss to Ireland and to literature. She was a lady of many talents, her last book 'The Four Winds of Eirinn' is fragrant with musical verse, which reveal the passion and spirituality of one of the sweetest singers the Irish Revival movement produced.*

# THE WEST'S ASLEEP

When all beside a vigil keep.
The West's asleep! the West's asleep -
Alas! and well may Erin weep
When Connacht lies in slumber deep.
There lake and plane smile fair and free,
'Mid rocks their guardian chivalry.
Sing, Oh! let man learn liberty
From crashing wind and lashing sea.

That chainless wave and lovely land
Freedom and nationhood demand;
Be sure the great God never planned
For slumb'ring slaves a home so grand.
And long a brave and haughty race
Honoured and sentinelled the place.
Sing, Oh! not even their son's disgrace
Can quite destroy their glory trace.

For often, in O'Connor's van,
To triumph dashed each Connacht clan,
And fleet as deer the Normans ran
Thro' Corlieu's Pass and Ardrahan;
And later times saw deeds as brave,
And glory guards Clanricarde's grave,
Sing, Oh! they died their land to save
At Aughrim's slopes and Shannon's wave.

And if, when all a vigil keep,
The West's asleep! the West's asleep!
Alas! and well may Erin weep
That Connacht lies in slumber deep.
But, hark! a voice like thunder spake,
The West's awake! the West's awake!
Sing Oh! hurrah! let England quake,
We'll watch till death for Erin's sake!

*Thomas Davis (1814 - 1845)*

*A rousing poem of Ireland in days of yore, of Irish history and mighty warriors, Connacht was at that time presumed to be inactive. They were reminded of their past glories and fighting clans. At the end of the poem they take up the sword again, and fight for Ireland.*

# THE OLD LAND

Ah kindly and sweet we must love thee, perforce!
The disloyal, the coward alone would not love thee;
Oh, mother of heroes! strong mother! soft nurse!
We are thine while the the large clouds swim onward above thee!
By thy ever blue that draw heaven so near;
By thy cliffs, by thy lakes, by thine ocean-lulled highlands!
And more by thy records disastrous and dear,
The shrines on thy headlands, the cells in thine islands!

Ah well sings the thrush by Lixnau and Triagh-li!
Ah well breaks the wave upon Umbhall and Brandon!
Thy breeze o'er the uplands blows clement and free,
And o'er fields once his own which the hind must now abandon,
A caitiff the noble who draws from thy plains
His all, yet reveres not the source of his greatness;
A clown and a serf, mid his boundless domains,
His spirit consumes in the prison of his straightness!

Through the cloud of its pathos thy face is more fair:
In old time thou wert sun-clad: the gold robe thou worest;
To thee the heart turns as the deer to its lair
Ere she dies, her first bed in the gloom of the forest.
Our glory, our sorrow, our mother! Thy God
In thy worst dereliction forsook but to prove thee:
Blind, blind as the blindworm; cold, cold as the clod,
Who seeing thee, see not, possess, but not love thee!

*Aubrey De Vere (1814-1902)*

*Another moving poem about Heroes, cowards, sorrow, and olden times in Ireland.*

*'Lixnau, Traigli' = Lixnaw and Tralee in Co Kerry, 'Umbhall' = West of Mayo.*
*Caitiff = coward, craven.*

# THIS IS MY OWN MY NATIVE LAND

Breathes there a man, with soul so dead,
Who never to himself hath said,
'This is my own, my native land !'
Whose heart hath ne'er within him burn'd,
As home his footsteps he hath turn'd
From wandering on a foreign strand !
If such there breathe, go mark him well ;
For him no minstrel raptures swell ;
High though his titles, proud his name,
Boundless his wealth as wish can claim ;
Despite those titles, power, and pelf,
The wretch, concentred all in self,
Living, shall forfeit fair renown,
And, doubly dying, shall go down
To the vile dust, from whence he sprung,
Unwept, unhonur'd, and unsung.

*Sir Walter Scott (1771-1832)*

*Son of an Edinburgh attorney. Started his career in Law, and then turned to Literature. One of his early publications 'Lay of the Last Minstrel' in 1805 made him a great poetical favourite of that time. In 1814 he gave up poetry, and started writing novels. In 1826 his publishers went bankrupt, leaving him with a liability One Hundred and Forty Seven Thousand pounds , he spent the rest of his life paying off this enormous amount.*

# THE LITTLE BLACK ROSE

The Little Black Rose shall be red at last;
What made it black but the March wind dry,
And the tear of the widow that fell on it fast?
It shall redden the hills when June is nigh!

The Silk of the Kine shall rest at last;
What drove her forth but the dragon fly?
In the golden vale she shall feed full fast,
With her mild gold horn and her, slow dark eye.

The wounded wood-dove lies dead at last!
The pine long bleeding, it shall not die!
This song is secret. Mine ear it passed
In a wind o'er the plain at Athenry.

*Aubrey De Vere*

*The Little Black Rose. This poem is a lament for the sorrows of Ireland. The Little Black Rose, Kathaleen Ny- Houlahan, My Dark Rosaleen, or Roisin Dubh, The Silk of the Kine, ect are some of the mystic names used by Irish poets For Ireland.*

# THE EXILE'S DEVOTION

I'd rather be a bird that sings
Above the martyr's grave,
Than fold in fortune's cage my wings
And feel my soul a slave;
I'd rather turn one simple verse
True to the Gaelic ear,
Then sapphic odes I might rehearse
With senates listening near.

Oh, native land! dost ever mark
When the world's is drown'd
Betwixt the day-light and the dark,
A wandering solemn sound
That on the western wind is borne
Across the dewy breast?
It is the voice of those who mourn
For thee, far in the west!

For them and theirs I oft essay
Your ancient art of Song,
And often sadly turn away,
Deeming my rashness wrong;
For well I ween, a loving will
Is all the art I own
Ah me could love suffice for skill
What triumphs I had known!

My native land! my native land!
Live in my memory still!
Break on my brain, ye surges grand!
Stand up, mist cover'd hill
Still on the mirror of the mind
The scenes I love, I see;
Would I could fly on the western wind,
My native land to thee!

*Thomas D'Arcy McGee (1825-1868)*

*Born in Carlingford Co Louth. He was a very successful journalist in America, He was editor of the 'Boston Pilot'. His denouncement of the Fenian Movement in Canada, where he had settled, led to his assassination in Ottawa in 1868. He wrote this very touching and heartfelt poem, about his love for his native land.*

# EXILE OF ERIN

There came to the beach a poor Exile of Erin,
The dew on his thin robe was heavy and chill:
For his country he sighed, when at twilight repairing
To wander alone by the wind beaten hill.
But the day star attracted his eye's sad devotion,
For it rose o'er his own native isle of the ocean,
Where once, in the fire of his youthful emotion,
He sang the bold anthem of Erin go bragh.


Sad is my fate! said the heart-broken stranger,
The wild deer and wolf to a covert can flee;
But I have no refuge from famine and danger,
A home and a country remain not to me.
Never again in the green sunny bowers,
Where my forefathers lived shall I spend the sweet hours,
Or cover my harp with the wild woven flowers,
And strike to the numbers of Erin go bragh!


Erin my country! though sad and forsaken,
In dreams I revisit thy sea-beaten shore;
But alas! in a fair foreign land I awaken,
And sigh for the friends who can meet me no more!
Oh cruel fate!wilt thou never replace me
In a mansion of peace where no perils can chase me?
Never again shall my brothers embrace me?
They died to defend me, or live to deplore!

Where is my cabin-door, fast by the wild wood
Sisters and sire! Did ye weep for its fall?
Where is the mother that looked on my childhood?
And where is the bosom friend, dearer than all?
Oh, my sad heart! Long abandoned by pleasure,
Why did it dote on a fast fading treasure?
Tears like the rain-drop may fall without measure,
But rapture and beauty they cannot recall.


Yet all its sad recollection suppressing,
One dying wish my lone bosom can draw:
Erin! an exile bequeaths thee his blessing!
Land of my forefathers! Erin go bragh!
Buried and cold, when my heart stills her motion,
Green be thy fields sweetest isle of the ocean!
And thy harp-striking bards sing aloud with devotion
Erin mavournin! – Erin go bragh!

*Thomas Cambell (1777-1844)*

*A native of Glasgow, Cambells fame will rest on his lyrics and loving Celtic nature. His Exile of Erin is a lovely sad and sentimental Irish poem.*

# RICH AND RARE WERE THE GEMS SHE WORE

Rich and rare were the gems she wore
And a bright gold ring on her wand she bore;
But, o'h her beauty was far beyond
Her sparkling gems or snow-white wand.

Lady, dost thou not fear to stray,
So lone and lovely, through this bleak way?
Are Erin's sons so good or so cold,
As not to be tempted by woman of gold?

Sir Knight I feel not the least alarm,
No son of Erin will offer me harm:
For, though they love women and golden store,
Sir Knight! they love honour and virtue more.

On she went with her maiden smile
In safety lighted her round the green isle;
And blest forever is she who relied
Upon Erin's honour and Erin's pride.

*Thomas Moore (1780-1852)*

*Born in Dublin educated at Trinity College. One of Irelands leading poets. His 'Irish Melodies' are the best of his works and will always remain the most popular. Amongst his best poems, 'Rich and rare were the Gems she wore.' A story of honour, chivalry, and virtue in days of yore.*

# THE BOLD FENIAN MEN

Oh see who comes over the red blossomed heather,
Their green banners kissing the pure mountain air,
Heads erect, eyes to front, stepping proudly together,
Freedom sits throned on each proud spirit there.
While down the hill twining, their blessed steel shining
Like rivers of beauty they flow through each glen ;
From mountain and valley tis liberty's rally
Out and make way for the bold Fenian men !

Our prayers and our tears have been scoffed and derided,
The've shut out God's sunlight from spirit and mind,
Our foes were united and we were divided,
We met and they scattered us all to the wind.
But once more returning within our veins burning
The fires that illumined dark Aherlow's glen ;
We raise the old cry anew, Slogan of Con and Hugh
Out and make way for the bold Fenian men.

We've men from the Nore, from the Suir, and the Shannon,
Let tyrants come forth, we'll bring force against force
Our pen is the sword and our voice is the cannon,
Rifle for rifle, and horse against horse,
We've made the false Saxon yield many a red battle field ;
God on our side we will triumph again
Oh pay them back woe for woe, strike them back blow for blow
Out and make way for the bold Fenian men.

*Michael Scanlan (1836-1908)*

*A stirring battle song from the Fenian days, another fine example of Michael Scanlan's Great Irish poems.*
*He also wrote amongst others, 'Limerick is beautiful', 'A day in Erin', The Jacket's Green' and many more*
*wonderful Irish poems. He was born in Limerick.*

# BANTRY BAY

As I'm sitting all alone in the gloaming,
It might have been but yesterday
That we watched the fisher sails all homing
Till the little herring fleet at anchor lay ;
Then the fisher girls with baskets swinging
Came running down the old stone way,
Ev'ry lassie to her sailor boy was singing
A welcome back to Bantry Bay.

Then we heard the piper's sweet note tuning,
And all the lassies turned to hear,
As they mingled with a soft voice crooning,
Till the music floated down the wooden pier,
'Save you kindly, colleens all,' said the piper,
Hands across and trip it while I play"
And the joyous sound song of merry dancing
Stole softly over Bantry Bay.

As I'm sitting all alone in the gloaming,
The shadows of the past draw near,
And I see the loving faces all around me
That used to glad the old brown pier ;
Some have gone on their last lov'd homing,
Some are left, but they are old and grey,
And we're waiting for the tide in the gloaming,
To sail upon the great highway,
To that land of rest unending,
All peacefully from Bantry Bay.

*James A Molloy*

*Bantry Bay is situated in the South West corner of Ireland where the Gulf Stream runs along the coast, it is set amid beautiful scenery of rugged mountains and hills, and semi-tropical plants grow in profusion in the area. The Bay is one of the finest deep-water bays in the World. It is about 35 miles long 7 miles wide and 40 fathoms deep. The biggest naval battle in Irish History was fought there on 1st of May 1698, when a heavily escorted French fleet defeated an English battle fleet during the Williamite wars. The French attempted to invade Ireland in 1796 but were foiled by a great storm that raged in the area over Christmas at that time. The English North Atlantic Battle fleet consisting of about 35 Warships and 20,000 sailors visited Bantry on a regular basis from about 1904 until the end of World War one in 1918.*

# THE LONDONDERRY AIR

*(Danny Boy)*

O Danny Boy the pipes the pipes are calling
From glen to glen and down the mountain side,
The summers gone and all the roses dying,
Tis you, tis you, must go and I must bide

But come Ye back when Summer's in the meadow,
Or if the valley's hushed and white with snow
Tis I'll be here in sunshine or in shadow,
For Danny Boy, oh Danny Boy, I love you so.

And when you come and all the flowers are dying
Then if I'm dead and dead I well may be,
Oh come and find the spot where I am lying,
And kneel and say an Ave there for me.

And I shall hear your soft feet tread above me
And o'er my grave the earth will warmer be,
And I will hear you whisper that you love me,
Then I will sleep in peace until you come to me.

*This is a beautiful heart-rending song that is loved and sung all over the world. There are many versions as to where this wonderful Irish melody originated. It is said that it was first heard played by a blind wandering fiddler in Limavady, Co Derry, near the banks of Lough Foyle in 1851. There was a lady by the name of Jane Ross who was a musician, staying there at that time, she was enchanted by the air he was playing, his name was Jimmy McCurry. She asked him to play the air again and wrote the music as he played. It was then called The Londonderry Air. As to the eventual title 'Danny Boy' and the lyrics, they were not written for some time afterwards. There is a lot of speculation and controversy as to who wrote them, it is generally accepted that an English laywer and noted lyric writer Fred Weatherly was the person who wrote the lyrics of 'Danny Boy'.*

*As to the interpretation I have always assumed that it was the story of a young Irishman, leaving his home and broken-hearted Mother to emigrate to America during the awful times of the famines of the 1840s.*

# PART THREE

# Memories of an Exile

## By

## Sean Kelly

# 452 AD

St Patrick came to Ireland
And blessed our native land,
He held the three leafed shamrock
In his sacred hand.
It became our emblem
Throughout the dreary years
It gave us faith and courage when we feared!
And now we love and revere him to this present day
We bless the name of Patrick
When we kneel to pray.

## Good Friday 10-4-1014 AD

Brave Brian Boru died that Easter day
On Clontarf's shining sand,
He beat the cruel invader
Despoiler of our land!
He gave his life for Ireland
He went to God with pride,
For Erin's hope
For Erin's name
Our noble hero died.

# 1-5-1170

False Dermot knelt on Wexford's shore
And kissed the Norman's hand,
And welcomed them
To share and plunder our beloved land.
They ravished our poor Country
For nigh on nine hundred years,
And for our lovely island
We had naught but tears.

# 4-9-1607

Two noble earls from Ulster
O'Neill and O'Donnell too,
Fought the invader bravely
And to Erin's cause were true.
At Kinsale town against Mountjoy
They fought their last brave fight
And with their Chieftains and followers
Left Erin in their flight.
They fought for Europe's armies
For many a lonely year
And lie with the brave
In foreign fields!
With no Irish prayer to cheer

# 15-08-1649

Cruel Cromwell came to Ireland
With his murderous Roundhead band,
And wrote his name in infamy
Throughout our native land.
He slaughtered maimed and tortured
Man woman and child alike,
He called his actions Gods work
As he put them to the pike.
But he will rue his cruelty
When he faces his God on high,
But the innocents of Ireland
Will never never die.

# MAY 1798

In 98 we fought again
With brave Father Murphy to lead,
And nearly freed our native land
With many a gallant deed.

We triumphed at Camolin
At Ross and Wexfords plain,
And the green fields of Shelmalier
We covered with foemen slain.

We beat them at Enniscorty
And at the Harrow too,
And their torture and their infamy,
We made the foemen rue.

We bravely fought at Vinegar Hill
And for our Country died.
And when they talk of 98
They remember us with pride.

# 1800s

The Fenians came and tried again
To free us from our chains.
They sent them to Van Damiens land
Far from their loves and bairns,
They sent them over the Southern Seas
In fetters and in chain;
Never to see their native home
Or the ones they loved again!

# Easter 1916

Then Patrick Pearse and his gallant band
Fought bravely to free their beloved land,
They died on the streets of Dublin
And challenged England's might,
In the General Post Office and outposts
For five long days and nights.

Then England took their cruel revenge
And wiped our leaders out,
Then from the people of Ireland
There came a mighty shout,
Murder our men you have lit a flame
A flame that will never die,
And we will free our native land
And the graves where our heroes lie!

# 1919-1921

Our brave young men they rose again
And lifted the banner of freedom,
They fought England to a standstill
With the bravest of the brave to lead them!

They fought the brave fight for liberty
They gave their lives for you,
Collins and brave Barry the fearless Bruga too,
Fought the long battle for Ireland
Fought with heart and hand,
After many years of conflict!
Freed their native land.

# September 1921

After nine hundred long years
Now you are gone never to be returning,
Ireland forgives but never forgets
The murder the pillage the burning.

# A CHILDHOOD DREAM

Isle of childhood memories,
Isle of childhood dreams,
Isle of what might have been
If the future could be seen.

What could be seen but never was,
Now in the misty past,
For life won't wait and time flies by,
And mortals breathe their last!

But, Oh! to walk in childhood's time,
And have the chance once more,
Never to leave one's native home,
And walk on foreign shores.

But we were children of despair
Driven from our land by cruel unfeeling rulers,
A smug self- centered band.
They drove us in our thousands to leave our native shore,
Never to walk on the green fields of home
Exiles for ever more!

So children of Ireland's exiles
Remember your forefather's land,
Never forget your heritage and for what you stand,
Love your Mother Ireland a country fair and green,
Said by bards and poets the finest ever seen!

# IRELAND

Beautiful Island far away,
Emerald of the sea,
Land of my forefathers in days of yore,
But always home to me.

Land of lofty mountains,
And rivers shining bright,
Land of myth and legends,
And Banshees in the night.

Land of saints and scholars,
And famous heroes too,
Land where the three leafed Shamrock,
Is kissed by the morning dew.

Land of happy people
No more in foreign chains,
Laughing in the sunlight,
A nation once again.

# WHY?

Why did we leave our native land
To work in foreign fields?
Why did we fight for alien kings
And let our homeland bleed?

Why did we build their cities great
While Ireland bled and died
Under the rule of foreign Kings
Whose cruelty patriots defied?

If only we stayed and fought with them,
The bravest of the brave,
Our lovely land by strangers
Would not have been enslaved.

At last our land is free again
And over our country flies
The flag of our pride,
White, orange and green,
For which our heroes died.

No more will our children leave Erin's shore
To work in foreign lands,
But will prosper in the freedom
Carved by patriot's hands.

# INNISFREE

On the broad Atlantic ocean
In the shimmering Celtic Sea,
Stands a lovely verdant island
That is known as Innisfree.
It had its share of torment,
It had its share of pain,
And now it proudly stands alone
A nation once again.

An example to all others
Of how to build and make
A future for our children
And good lives for them to shape,
Be true to God and love the old
And never fear the truth,
Sow the seeds of honesty
And profit by its fruit.

This was taught by fearless men
Over many many years,
They shaped and made our future
And banished all our fears,
And so we stand together
In our beloved land,
And live in peace and harmony,
A blithe and carefree band.

# THE WILD GEESE 1691

*(A Lament for the Irish Jacobites)*

The wild geese flew on a cold wintry day,
They cursed the invader they fought in the fray,
They lost the long fight for their native land,
And with Sarsfield they formed a valiant band!

They fought and they died as the Irish Brigade
From the foothills of Russia to the streets of Belgrade,
They carried before them their banners of green,
And a more gallant army never was seen!

They fought the Frank and they fought the Hun,
And drank and caroused when the fighting was done,
On the battlefields of Europe they sleep with the brave,
The chieftains and men of the Irish Brigade.

# THE LONELY EMIGRANT

Sad is the stranger
Far from his home
Which he left long ago
To wander and roam
No wife or no children
To greet him each day
All his hopes and dreams
Have long faded away.

He sits every night
In a  cold lonely room
He sits all alone
In despair and in gloom
He has long lonely hours
To dream and to rue
The homeland he left
And the loved ones he knew.

He left them one day
And sailed far away
From the land of his birth
At the dawn of the day.

# IRELAND'S LAMENT

My sons and daughters have gone far away
From their homes and the land of their birth,
No more will my hills and valleys ring
With their laughter their songs and their mirth!

The false promises and lies of heartless men,
Sent them away in their hordes,
They were cheated and robbed of their future
And the homeland that they adored!

They slaved and they toiled in foreign fields,
They never forgot their home,
And prayed for the day they could return
Never again to roam,
But for some that dream never came true
And in foreign fields they lie,
Far from the land they loved so dear
Under an alien sky!

But that day has now gone
And my children are here never again to roam,
And the laughter and song resounds through the hills
From thousands of Irish homes.

So pray for the emigrants far from our land
And hope in Gods arms they sleep,
And forgive them that caused my children to roam,
For what they sow they shall reap.